Little Money Street

Little Money Street

*In Search of Gypsies and Their Music in the
South of France*

Fernanda Eberstadt

ALFRED A. KNOPF
NEW YORK
2006

THIS IS A BORZOI BOOK
PUBLISHED BY ALFRED A. KNOPF

Copyright © 2006 by Fernanda Eberstadt

www.aaknopf.com

Knopf, Borzoi Books, and the colophon are registered trademarks of
Random House, Inc.

Library of Congress Cataloging-in-Publication Data

Eberstadt, Fernanda, [date].
Little money street : in search of Gypsies and their music in the south of
France / Fernanda Eberstadt.— 1st ed.
p.   cm.
ISBN 0-375-41116-X
1. Romanies—France—Perpignan—Social life and customs.   2. Romanies—
France—Perpignan—Music.   3. Romanies—France—Perpignan—Economic
conditions.   I. Title.

DX227.E34 2006
305.891'497044—dc22
2005044139

Manufactured in the United States of America

First Edition

For Maud and Theo

Acknowledgments

Many people taught me about Roussillon and Catalans, about Gypsies and Gypsy music, about what it means to be an outsider in the developed world; others helped refine the ideas that are in this book; others made the writing of it much more pleasant.

First thanks to my friends in Roussillon: to Georges de Massia, who with impetuous generosity, daring, and insight has created at Mas de Lacroix not just delicious wines, but a stronghold of solidarity and good fellowship. To our neighbors and dear friends, Sylvie Laporte and Olivier Gross, for many days and nights of talk. To Monique Souberan de Saint-Prix, inspiring soul mate, attentive reader. To Dr. Andrée Morcrette, a doctor and fellow mother healing Gypsy mothers and their children, for her kind and forthright discussions of how it feels to be a Catalan in French Catalonia. To Hajiba Mohib for hot meals, warm friendship, spicy conversation, and invaluable insights, and to her partner Frederic Guillem for leading me to Moïse and Diane. To Garth Beattie, for his open door and fearsome tales, who introduced me to Gypsy music and its makers.

Above all, this book belongs to Diane Meziani, Moïse Espinas, and their children Kevin and Marlon; to Diane's sister and her children and to their extended family, who have sheltered and welcomed me, and awakened me to worlds beyond my imagining—thank you, beloved friends, with all my heart.

Little Money Street is dedicated to Maud and Theo, who lived it, but its secret hero is Alastair Bruton, who had the strange idea that marriage could be more fun than a bank heist, and who inspired and shared these adventures.

In New York, all thanks to my agent Lynn Nesbit, for her wisdom, faith, and indomitable good cheer. And to the best of editors, Bob Gottlieb and Shelley Wanger.

Thanks to Pierre Hodgson, as always.

Several people's names have been changed, at their request, but otherwise, the stories are as I heard them.

Little Money Street

Chapter One

1

Diane isn't much of a cook. She lives off Marlboros and black coffee, and I have never in all these years seen Diane offer food to her husband or children. Every time I visit, she greets me with the ritual inducements to eat, drink (that is, have a cigarette, a glass of Coke, some Cheez Doodles). But only once have I eaten a meal at Diane's house.

Diane, I think, was feeling a little guilty about the Yuri Buenaventura concert. Yuri Buenaventura is a Latin American salsa star who has a passionate following in southern France, where we live. This spring, his European tour included a gig at Perpignan's Mediator. "I'm gonna *die* if I don't hear Yuri live," Diane had been saying for months.

If you spend much time with Diane, it's hard to resist wanting to be her fairy godmother. Six weeks in advance, I bought four tickets to Yuri Buenaventura's concert, thinking, Alastair and I, Diane and her husband, Moïse, could all go. "Moïse" is pronounced "Mo-EEZ." But Diane and Moïse are Gypsies, and married couples' double-dating is not Gypsies' idea of fun.

Diane asks Moïse if he'd like to come along to the concert.

Moïse, at twenty-eight, is one of the greatest Gypsy singers in France. But Moïse has a complicated attitude toward music, as if his own gift lies in a state of untaught purity that might be defiled either by too much use or by exposure to other people's music. Moïse scowls. "No way, woman. It'll be full of Gypsies."

"No, it won't."

"Sure it will: Gypsies love salsa. Every lousy little Gypsy in Perpignan will be stuffed tight in that place, you know it."

If Moïse doesn't want to go hear Yuri, does that mean he'll stay home with the children?

This is when a familiar game begins, the funny-sad cat-and-mouse routine of a couple who have been married since they were seventeen, and know in their sleep how to drive each other mad.

"When's the concert?" Moïse asks.

Thursday.

"Thursday, Thursday, Thursday." Moïse furrows his brow, as if "Thursday" were a friend of Diane's whose face he can't quite place. Finally, he relents. "Fine—I'll stay home, rent a video for the kids."

At the good news, Diane explodes into a shimmering volcano of joy. She jumps to her feet, shoves her favorite Yuri tape into the player and rolls the volume to the max, grabs me by the hands, and salsas around the apartment, a gap-toothed grin on her face. She picks up her cell phone, presses autodial to call her sister, her nieces, and her cousins to gloat, for the Yuri concert is famously sold out. "Christine? You'll never guess where me and Fernande are going Thursday night. . . ."

A dozen times already I've made such plans with Diane, who is permanently crazy-itching-mad to burst out of the house, to flee the confines of being a stay-at-home mother in a culture that places pathological restrictions on women. Diane's ambitions are not really so extreme. She wants to go for a drink at Boca Boca, a chic Cuban-style bar, with me and two "French" (i.e., non-Gypsy) friends. Diane needs this phalanx of palefaces: when she tries going to Boca Boca with her niece Tanya and an Arab schoolfriend of Tanya's, they are turned away at the door. She wants to go out for her birthday to a seaside disco with me and a bunch of girl-friends. Not so much to ask. Just a girls' night out, no men, because it is only with other women that you can relax and enjoy yourself. My working-class "French" friends make the same assumption: if you want a good time, it's girls with the girls and boys with the boys.

Moïse will stay home with the kids, because Moïse is open-minded; he allows his wife to go out, as long as she is properly chaperoned and goes to a place where she won't be spotted by other Gypsies. We are going to lie to Moïse—we are going to tell him we are going to a concert at the Mediator, when in fact we are going to a disco at Canet Plage. (The difference to me appears negligible, but subterfuge is an essential element to the bust-out: if you didn't have to lie to your spouse about what you'd done, it couldn't have been any fun.)

Every couple of months, Diane and I concoct such Nights to Howl. But something always gets in the way, usually at about eight o'clock on the destined evening. An obstacle, which to me seems insignificant, after a brief acquaintance with Diane comes to be painfully predictable. Diane's "fate"—the ill-health and fatigue that are the bodily expressions of her unhappiness—intervenes.

Yuri Buenaventura Night, when I ring Diane's buzzer, the shutters are barred and the lights are out. Her sister Linda, who lives in the apartment upstairs, explains over the intercom that Diane and Moïse have taken the baby to the doctor. Even though Baby Marlon's had a cold all week, it's only just at eight that evening that they've decided to get the doctor to check him out.

When I next hear from Diane, she asks me if I videotaped the concert for her, and when I say no, she invites me to Sunday lunch.

2

Moïse and Diane live in a bright, whitewashed modern apartment building on the Boulevard Aristide Briand, one stretch of the pentangular road that engirdles the medieval city center of Perpignan. Across the street from their building begins St. Jacques, the prime Gypsy neighborhood of the city.

St. Jacques, a ramshackle slum, is five hundred yards from Moïse and Diane's door. Their window overlooks the street on which all of Diane's and most of Moïse's relatives live, but to their minds, they have left St. Jacques far behind.

Boulevard Aristide Briand is a dusty commercial thoroughfare, but its stores—a motorcycle showroom, a string of real estate agents, doctors' offices—suggest a population whose purchasing power is royal compared to the squalid penury of St. Jacques. In Moïse and Diane's immaculate apartment, the furniture is showroom-new. Today, on this particular Sunday noon, it's filled with Moïse, Diane, their

sons Kevin and Marlon, Diane's sister Linda and her two
children, me, and two other non-Gypsy friends of Diane's—
Marie, a grandmotherly woman who is a human rights activ-
ist, and Marie's friend Nicole, a surgeon's widow.

Diane and Linda squabble over what to serve their guests
before lunch: Diane offers us a *digestif;* "Idiot," says Linda,
"that's for *after* the meal." Diane instead serves us Malibu,
a coconut liqueur, and whiskey. Moïse obligingly puts out a
plate of cookies; "Idiot," says Diane, "that's for dessert, you
need to give them salted peanuts."

For lunch, Diane orders take-out pizza. The thing I
remember chiefly from Diane's lunch party is the expression
on the pizza deliveryman's face.

I know the man already: he runs the pizzeria across the
street from Diane's. When I take my children there, he spoils
and praises them: Americans in this area are a high-prestige
rarity.

Today I see another face. The pizzaman has obviously
come to the apartment not realizing that Gypsies live here
(Diane's surname is North African, the neighbors are all
"French"), and once the door has been locked and double-
bolted behind him, he looks as if he's been lured into Fort
Apache, the Bronx.

Straightaway there is the question in the air of are-we-
going-to-pay, and what's he going to do about it if we don't.
The bill is only about twelve dollars, as Diane—no eater
herself—has ordered two small pizzas for ten people, but neither she nor Moïse seem able to cover it, nor will they hear of
their guests' chipping in.

The pizzaman surveys us, one by one, with a contemp-
tuous smirk, fear disguised as a sneer. It's a look I see again
and again when I am with Gypsies, a look that gives me the

sense of being on the other side of the looking glass, of what it might be like to be an Undesirable in the developed Western world—the wrong color, the wrong religion, the wrong income bracket. When the pizzaman's gaze comes to me, he does an involuntary double take, as if he'd spotted a supposedly respectable neighbor soliciting in the red-light zone, before his expression once again hardens.

The showdown ends in a fumble of embarrassment. Diane produces a checkbook, but can't figure out how to fill out the check. "Give it to Marie," suggests Moïse, in a rare gesture of husbandly protectiveness.

Diane's friend Marie makes out the check, and the pizzaman escapes alive.

3

Diane and Moïse are both exhausted. *Fatigués, fatigués,* complains Diane.

Gypsies are night owls—even the women, who stay at home, watch television all night, and sleep as much of the day as they can.

Moïse, as usual, got home at five o'clock this morning. Moïse's band, Tekameli, was giving a concert outside Toulouse. Diane stayed up to let him in, and then got up two hours later when the baby awoke. But whereas Diane is stressed to black hysteria, Moïse is a calm sort of grouchy, like a bear awakening from the winter.

"Aren't you going to eat, Moïse?"

Moïse isn't going to eat; Moïse has only just crawled out of bed. In a couple of hours he'll get hungry, and then he'll grab something: his eating hours are permanently jet-lagged, he explains, apologetically.

Diane now raises the pizza knife, and thrusts it toward her husband's heart. "I haven't yet settled accounts with you, Mr. Espinas. I gave you a break because of Toulouse."

Two nights before—the night when she was supposed to go to Yuri Buenaventura but couldn't, because they had to take the baby to the doctor—Moïse had gone out afterward, and not come home until *eight the following morning.*

"He says he was at the movies," she explains, sardonically.

"It's true: I went to the cineplex at Rivesaltes," he insists. "Look, I've even got the ticket stub."

She examines it. "So what's that prove? You went to the nine p.m. show. *Then* what did you do till eight the next morning?"

He stands there, sleepy, but not a bit abashed.

She turns to her women friends. "You know what he tells me? He tells me, I was *enjoying nature.*"

The Rivesaltes cineplex is in a supermall right off the superhighway to Spain. There's a supersupermarket, a mega bowling alley, a McDonald's with an indoor playground the size of a college gym, the French equivalent of Home Depot, but not much in the way of nature, unless you count the Super-Mega-Hyper Pet Supply Shop. There is a perverse beauty to the idea of Moïse, an overgrown slum kid, enjoying nature in the flatlands mallscape in the middle of the night.

And Moïse, at this moment, is also enjoying the idea. He stoops to pick a slice of cold pizza from the box, but Diane stops him. "Look what a slob you're becoming. Didn't the doctor say you have to lose weight?"

Moïse is a handsome man who radiates a quiet comfortable sense of his own attractiveness, but he is indeed getting pudgy.

The women discuss Moïse's weight, and what is strange about the conversation is its air of irreversible doom. Everyone agrees that Moïse should take off twenty pounds, and yet it seems equally evident to them that he will instead continue to balloon.

Moïse stands above us, in a clinging black rayon T-shirt bedecked with a big gold crucifix, and a pair of black polyester stretch pants with a built-in buckle like an airplane seat belt, and he smiles a winning, baby-toothed smile.

No, no, he informs us happily, he has it all figured out: he is going to go to a health club where they give you massages! Now the gestures unroll, the salesman making his pitch, Moïse basking like a seal, luxuriating in his imagined weight-loss regime: he'll even swim a little in the health club swimming pool, just to get himself really relaxed for the massages! Moïse, in fact, can't swim, although he lives by the sea.

"He'll never do it," says Diane, darkly. "He'll go once, maybe, but never again."

Chapter Two

1

I'd been living outside Perpignan a year and a half before I finally managed to meet a Gypsy. My prolonged failure tells you a lot about the chasm between Gypsy lives and non-Gypsy lives in this otherwise rough-and-tumble Mediterranean border town.

Perpignan, the last city in France before you cross into Spanish Catalonia, is a major stop in one particular Gypsy homeland that reaches along the coast from the French Camargue down to Barcelona. Perpignan itself is said to have the largest Gypsy population of any city center in Western Europe, a population that first arrived here in the late Middle Ages, and has been settled since the Second World War.

Although Gypsies' ticklish relation to officialdom makes them understandably census-shy, it is estimated that as many as 5,000 of central Perpignan's 100,000-plus inhabitants are Gypsy. Five percent may not sound like much, but it's enough to swing a mayoral election in a town whose vote is fragmented among numerous political parties, none of which can command a majority. Which means that Perpignan may just be the only city in the world where politicians win elections by courting the Gypsy vote.

"Courting" is a euphemism: in fact, mayors of Perpignan for the last thirty years supposedly have *bought* the Gypsy vote, originally by handing out banknotes in the main square of St. Jacques, nowadays, it is said, with jobs, apartments, goods—a habit that's become something of a national scandal. And yet, what I discovered was that this largish and politically pivotal community was nonetheless inviolably cut off from mainstream "French" Perpignan.

Large gangs of Gypsies—boys in white zoot suits and slicked-back pompadours, or women in long black skirts and house slippers, pushing children in strollers—parade the downtown boulevards, at once startlingly conspicuous and ignored. Non-Gypsies venturing into the Gypsy neighborhoods of St. Jacques or Haut Vernet suffer the same conspicuous invisibility.

The Gypsies of Perpignan belong to clans that have been living in this corner of France since the early 1400s. They have been settled in the same neighborhoods—often the same houses and apartment buildings—since 1940, when the Vichy government outlawed nomadism. Yet if a Perpignan Gypsy wants to refer politely to a non-Gypsy, she calls him a *"Français."* (The word used among themselves is *paio,* the Spanish Romany equivalent of *gadjo.*) What does it mean to feel oneself and one's people so inassimilably alien to the surrounding majority?

All my life, I've been drawn to Gypsies. One of my earliest memories is of sitting at an outdoor café in Paris with my parents, and watching a ragged and immensely insolent boy, accompanied by two ladies in multicolored skirts, pass from table to table, asking for money. When the mysterious strangers disappeared around the corner, the world without them seemed unbearably pale and insipid.

Since then, wherever I've been, I've sought out Gypsies—Gypsies who run traveling circuses in Ireland, or sleep in the ruined Byzantine city walls in Istanbul, or camp on the beach in Palermo, or even live in a brownstone basement on the Upper West Side of Manhattan. And even though I long ago learned that Gypsy life is not "free," but on the contrary far more hierarchical and prohibition-bound than that of secular Westerners, still I've felt the same attraction to their intractable difference.

For a year and a half in Perpignan, I asked everyone I met about Gypsies. I heard all kinds of stories. Some were familiar—that Gypsies dealt drugs, that they taught their children to steal, and that the Gypsy population of St. Jacques was massively infected with AIDS—stories combining three favorite themes about unwelcome minorities: they are rich, they are poor, and they are bearers of infectious diseases. Other legends were particularly local: that the widespread obesity you saw among Perpignan Gypsies was a deliberate ploy to get extra disability payments from the government, that each family fattened up one of its children, Hansel-style, with this end in mind.

Everybody had an anecdote about Gypsies, but nobody had actually met one. My friend Samia, a sociology student who lived in the heart of St. Jacques, told me, "Every day I pass the same old men playing cards, the same old ladies sitting on chairs in the street. We come home at two in the morning on a summer's night, and the little boys are zooming up and down on their scooters. Usually, if you've got small children, people will say something to you, smile, offer the little girl a candy. Here, after all these years, people still look right through us as if we were ghosts.

"Once only has a Gypsy spoken to me. At an open-air concert in the square, a group of teenaged girls approached us, and the boldest one shouted, Do you believe in God? I said, No, I don't. They were horrified! I said, Besides, I'm Muslim, I don't have the same God as you. They said, There is only one God, Jesus, and they fled as if I were the devil!"

2

In the autumn of 1998, my husband and I, with our two small children, came to live in Roussillon, the province of which Perpignan is the capital. My husband was writing a book about the decline of religion in modern Europe, and was looking for somewhere half to hole up in, half to base it upon. We rented a nineteenth-century country house outside Perpignan belonging to an old local family now transplanted to Paris.

I hadn't in the least bit intended to move to rural France. I wrote novels that were set in contemporary Manhattan, which was where our older child was due to start school that fall. But, having been landed in Roussillon kicking and screaming, I started to explore, and found I liked the place better than almost anywhere I'd been.

Roussillon is at the eastern end of the Pyrenees, where they dip into the Mediterranean Sea. Spain ceded Roussillon to France only in 1659. Today it is part of an amalgamated *région* called Languedoc-Roussillon, but once you cross from the sunny godless prosperous towns of the Languedoc into Roussillon, you realize that you are no longer in mainland

France, although where exactly you are is a more puzzling question.

Barcelona is the closest major city. Catalan is the official second language of Roussillon, and its natives, who are French Catalan, call the province "Northern Catalonia," in the conceit that there is still one Catalan homeland, running from Spanish Tarragona to the French fort of Salses, a conceit not widely shared by Spanish Catalans, who consider their French cousins treacherous hicks. The Gypsies who live in Roussillon, too, are for the most part Catalan Gypsies, whose language (they call it *Gitan*) is Catalan hybridized with *Kalo,* a Spanish dialect of Romany, although there are also Andalusian Gypsies who speak a similarly souped-up Spanish, as well as a smaller, still nomadic population of the Manush or Sinti Gypsy groups.

Many habits you might think of as Spanish still characterize Roussillon—inflections which can still be found in Palermo or Naples, cities that the Catalan-Aragonese also ruled. In religion, there's a counterreformational tendency to linger on the gorier aspects of saints' martyrdoms and Jesus' passion, a tradition of home shrines as intricate as voodoo altars, containing what are said to be fragments of saints' thighbones, vials of saints' dried blood.

The Catalan country house in which we live, on a vineyard by the sea, has a number of such *capellettas,* including a glass bell jar containing a black Madonna affixed with handwritten ex-votos, locks of hair, a wedding photograph. On visiting the mountaintop castle of an old lady belonging to an ancient French Catalan family, I was startled to see two legs protruding horizontally from a second-floor doorway: a chapel, in which a life-sized Virgin Mary, clothed in embroidered robes, lay on a bier.

With religion comes a Spanish-style sweet tooth. The most elegant tea shop in Perpignan is Espi, founded by a family of Spanish *pieds noirs* from the Spanish Algerian colony of Oran, who—caught between Algerian independence and Franco's rule at home—sought refuge in southern France in the early '60s, and who cater to fellow Spaniards' craving for bitter-black hot chocolate and for slabs of almond-honey paste.

In Perpignan's characteristic time warp, Espi's tea room is crowded every afternoon not just with old ladies, but also with teenagers, married couples, and middle-aged men who in more entrepreneurial climes might be at sales conferences or board meetings, but who here find themselves at four o'clock on Wednesday devouring almond-flour pastries off lace paper doilies.

3

Roussillon, for a prime strip of Mediterranean coastline, is oddly desolate. Few French northerners you meet have ever been to Roussillon, and many have never heard of it. A childhood friend of mine from Paris, when I told her I was living here, crowed, half-amused, half-horrified, "But it's as if I told you I had moved to rural Tennessee!"

Yet Roussillon is a ridiculously beautiful place, when it isn't downright ugly. Its southern border is the Pyrenees, a dark-green mountain range forested in cork trees, punctuated by hot sulphur springs where the ancient Celts worshipped nymphs, and studded with tiny Romanesque chapels and hermitages founded by refugees from Muslim Spain.

The Pyrenees have never been very formidable as a natural frontier, either on the Atlantic coast, where Basques are found on both sides, or down here, where the people are Catalans. These mountains, though steep, have wide-open passes, and for thousands of years, hunters, herders, smugglers, and religious fugitives from Cathars to Jews have crisscrossed this theoretical border in a two-way traffic.

On the French side, the Pyrenees descend into wide orcharded plains carved by the big rivers of the Tet and the Tech: lush valleys where farmers grow the cherries, apricots, and peaches that used to be prized in Paris as the "first fruits" of the season, but which have since been undercut by Spain and Morocco.

To the north, where Roussillon borders the Languedoc, runs a drier, whiter mountain range with limestone crags called the Corbieres, topped by ruined Cathar castles and riddled with caves, in one of which, thirty years ago, was discovered the 450,000-year-old skeleton of a young hunter known as "Tautavel man." Tautavel man's post-mortem fate is a poignant exemplum of our mixed nature. Paleontologists tell us that his brains were scooped out and eaten, while his skull was used as a mask in what they conjecture was religious pantomime.

The chalky moonscape surrounding Tautavel amphibianizes east into a salt marsh called the Salanque that today is artichoke fields, horse ranches, and vineyards—including the one on which we live. A paradox of honky-tonk beauty, in which flamingo-haunted lagoons coexist with Aqualands and trailer camps of Northern vacationers, a sub-industry that is boarded up ten months a year, and that off-season leaves these wetlands eerily deserted, the preserve of duck-hunters and gay cruisers.

History's few imprints on this littoral are scabrous. In February 1939, half a million defeated Spanish Republican fighters and their families poured across the Pyrenees into Roussillon, and were interned in concentration camps on the beaches, where many thousands died of cold, disease, and hunger. And on the salt plain, alongside the neon-glittery strip mall in which Moïse Espinas spent the night of the Yuri Buenaventura concert "enjoying nature," is the camp of Rivesaltes, where successive populations of Spanish Republican refugees, Roussillon Gypsies, and Jews from all over Europe were imprisoned in similarly murderous conditions. After the Allied invasion, 2,250 Jews were sent on to Auschwitz to be gassed.

There are hints that Roussillon's inhospitality has deep roots. At a conference on the history of the Jews in Roussillon, one participant told of a Turkish Jewish friend in whose family the legend had been passed down that in 1492, when their ancestors, expelled from Spain, sought refuge in Roussillon, the local Jews received them vilely. Geographical character runs steady. No surprise that in the last two presidential elections, the extreme right-wing National Front, a party which proposes expelling Arabs and Africans and sending Gypsies "back" to Spain, should have won in Roussillon one of its highest national scores.

The camp of Rivesaltes remains—crumbling barracks, their thin walls arctic in winter, baking in summer. In fact, in a staggering piece of official inhumanity, one portion of the zone *still* serves as an internment camp, housing immigrants (mainly Arab and African) facing deportation. Survivors of Rivesaltes recall, with a shudder, the Tramontane, the howling wind which flung skeletal prisoners off their feet and which still comes tearing down from the northwest two hundred days a year, and tends to turn one's lovely day at the beach into a blinding desert sandstorm.

4

Because the province of Roussillon has always been a strategic borderland, the region has retained a lost, no-man's-land quality. Its beauty is wild and forlorn, its monuments are military: watchtowers, forts, mountaintop castles.

You do not get the feeling here of a place where people have been settled, bustling, prosperous for unbroken millennia. Of Roussillon's two ruling cities of classical antiquity, Elne—née Illiberis—has been in sweet golden decline ever since its Celtic chiefs sided with Hannibal against Rome, while Ruscino, an Iberian city which in the seventh century B.C. was importing luxury goods from Etruria, Greece, and Asia Minor, mysteriously punked out early in the Roman Empire, and is today a mostly unexcavated bump on the outskirts of Perpignan.

The few classical remnants that have been unearthed attest to the area's Mediterranean spirit of *métissage*, or mixity: a deposit of lead votive prayers addressed to the local nymphs, the Niskae, were found by the thermal springs of Arles-sur-Tech (and lost, in 1901). These prayers were composed in a mixture of Celtic, street Latin, and Iberian (a non-Indo-European language which has not yet been fully cracked), and transliterated into a combination of Latin and Greek alphabets: then as now, the people of Roussillon were multilingual.

Roussillon's high times were the Middle Ages, when the province was divided into three or four fiefs, each ruled by its own dynasty of Catalan counts, who were secured in their privileges by the Carolingian Franks in exchange for keeping the Muslims at bay. The Middle Ages were a juicy time to have majored in. But looking around the windswept emptiness of Roussillon today, you sometimes get the impression that nothing much has happened here since 1300. Certain developments crucial for later socioeconomic well-being are missing from Roussillon's CV. Because it belonged to Castilian Spain until the mid-seventeenth century, Roussillon missed out on a period when the rest of what is now southern France was discovering Protestantism and the textile industry.

On the other hand, maybe because its plains were rich enough to keep boys on the farm, Roussillon never developed the seagoing expertise that made its Spanish cousins sailors, mercenaries, and traders famous from Constantinople to Cuba to the Philippines. The region instead has been characterized by a cross-eyed conservatism. During the French Revolution, its nobility raised a counterinsurgency whose aim was to reattach the province to Spain. (An ancestor of our landlord's was beheaded in downtown Perpignan after slipping back across the border from Spain to catch a glimpse of his young wife and children.) In the Industrial Age, Roussillon's leaders stuck to an all-agricultural policy, and nowadays their grandchildren continue to produce oceans of low-grade fruits and vegetables in a rock-bottom market, betting that they can survive on mounting subsidies till the day they sell out to developers.

Today, people from Perpignan find themselves looking at neighboring cities of the French *midi*, and thinking, like ambitious mothers, Why can't you be like Nîmes, whose Protestant manufacturers gave it a tradition of civic-mindedness and high culture, or Montpellier, which has had first-rate medical schools since the Middle Ages, or Toulouse, with its aerospace industry? A scholar of prehistoric

Roussillon, remarking upon the absence here of Paleolithic artwork compared with the riches found elsewhere in the French Pyrenees, wonders despairingly, "Were our Catalan ancestors of the Aurignacian or Magdalenian periods utterly impermeable to aesthetic emotion?"

Roussillon is like a child who was malnourished in the womb or deprived of oxygen too long at birth, a child who because he missed which formative stage of development— the Enlightenment? the Renaissance? the Roman Conquest? the Aurignacian Epoch?—can never now catch up, will always be half-savage, halting in speech, unable to do long division or tie his own shoelaces. Here, you progress from the seasonal camps of pre-Neanderthal hunters to the internment camps of the Second World War to the trailer camps of Scandinavian vacationers with terrifying rapidity.

5

"Y no niego que mi tierra / Es Perpinya de la Frontera" (And I don't deny my birthplace / Is Perpignàn de la Frontera), sings the young Gypsy musician Kanélé, sardonically likening his own hometown to Jerez de la Frontera, the Nashville of flamenco.

Perpignan, built on a series of bluffs overlooking the River Tet, is a maze of rough-paved streets that straggle up and down hills and ravines, alongside canals and filled-in streams. Street names are sometimes earthy, sometimes ethereal, sometimes terrifying, impregnated in a past that still seems nervously alive: Street of False Witnesses, Street of 15 Degrees, Street of the Great Fire, Dragon Street, Moon Street, Lantern Street, Street of the Three Days, Iron Hand

Street, Soap-Factory Street, Eel Street, Big Money Street, and the street whose name best describes the condition of most people I know in Perpignan, Little Money Street.

Because the city's so twisty, it's taken me years to grasp its overall layout, to divine how the rival quarters of St. Jacques or St. Mathieu sit in relation to each other. And still I steer topographically, navigating not by mental compass but by altimeter. If you want to get from Hell Street to Paradise Street, there are two hills to cross, and each time, you discover a hidden wonder: a circus school housed in the corner of the old arsenal; a club for harmonica-lovers.

Sometimes it seems that while Perpignan's uglinesses are plain to see, its treasures lie behind closed doors. This, of course, is the flip side of Mediterraneanness: that warm sun and forgiving soil have produced a closed people who live in darkness. It tells you a lot about the enduring hiddenness of "Perpinyà la Catalane" that only when the railroad came through in 1901 were its defensive walls finally dismantled—though long straggly chunks still survive. There are those who say that the rampart mentality endures here, and that it's a feature of the Catalans, a race, as one native reminds me drily, "not known for its openness or hospitality."

6

Exploring Perpignan, I found still intact an older, shabbier, weirder Europe of my childhood dreams, a Europe which I imagined to have been effaced by decades of postwar prosperity. Perpignan is a city where the old Adam has been neither demolished nor renovated, but survives, sooty, tumbledown, pungent, impenitently insalubrious.

What's conspicuous, initially, is an absence: when I first arrived, there were practically no chain stores. (Already, in six years, this is beginning to change.) Instead, in the red-marble arcades of Perpignan's grand shopping streets are nested a delirious proliferation of hat stores, glove stores, button stores, stores specializing in model-train parts, or terra-cotta figurines for crèches. There are an improbable number of mercers in downtown Perpignan, for this is a place where even young people still make their own clothes, where my doctor- or teacher-friends are amazed that I don't know how to darn the holes in my sweaters. On the poorer backstreets are artisans' workshops: chair-caners, piano-tuners, and guitar-stringers, as well as not one but three public scribes.

The open-air market at Place de la République is similarly specialized. There is a poulterer for fowl and eggs, different butchers for pork and for beef, and an assortment of foragers offering snails, wild asparagus, violets, and sorrel, including a trio of elderly Catalans—brother, sister, husband—who get cross if you want to buy too much of anything.

"What do you do with your sorrel, anyway?" the husband asks me. How you intend to cook your food is a common French question, occasion for choruses of competing recipes. French national self-confidence has taken a beating in the last century, between Vichy and Algeria, but food still remains a redeeming source of absolute value, a cultural lodestone. When people want to ask me about America, it's always, What do you eat for breakfast, lunch, and Christmas?

There are three possible answers to the husband's question. You can make soup with sorrel. You can cook it in an omelette. Or you can make a sauce for fish or chicken. I opt for the briefest.

"Soup. What do *you* do with it?"

"Nothing," he snorts with distaste. "I get rid of it."

It was in the market at Place de la République that I first encountered the old-fashioned rhythm of seasons. If you live in Roussillon, as opposed to northern Ontario, eating local isn't much of a constraint. But even so, seasons require a patience that I, a born Manhattanite used to strawberries for Christmas from Korean grocers, wasn't prepared for: *millas,* a slab of cornmeal made with butter, only appears once the nights freeze; no wild mushrooms without three days' rain, or sheep's cheese until the ewes have birthed, or tuna till Easter—an old and honorable decorum taken for granted by French housewives, although to Gypsies like Diane, living in a dichotomy of biblical-archaic and strip-mall modern, it's forgotten.

"How are your tomatoes?" asks a shopper.

Nicole, the vegetable lady, pulls a face. "You really want to eat a tomato in February?"

In the République market, there are more social pleasures, too. In the adjoining rue Paratilla, the rabbit-on-a-spit-seller serenades the fish lady with bawdy songs, and the ham-shop owner's many friends sit at outdoor tables in the cobblestoned sun, eating thin slices of *chamascado* served with bread rubbed in raw tomato. (It's part of Mediterranean laxness, the Sephardic spirit of rueful pragmatism that the Bodega del Jamon's best customer is the president of the synagogue.)

I've gone dancing with the blonde Algerian vegetable-seller and her bluestocking daughters. Their competitors in the neighboring stall, two quick mocking sisters from Provence, like to tease my husband. When he came shopping with a lady friend, they insisted on giving him a twenty-pound watermelon, to bring home as a consolation prize for me.

One day the rue Paratilla erupted when an elderly Arab pointed out to a black African lady that the rockfish she'd bought had just leaped out of her shopping basket and was flapping on the pavement. "And I always swore your fish was frozen!" M. Ferrer the ham-shop man crowed to Mireille the fishmonger.

What makes possible this survival of a more leisurely and convivial approach to commerce is poverty—not that Roussillon is poor in any worldwide sense—but let's say, the relative poverty of an undeveloped corner of an extremely rich country in which welfare benefits have been developed to a fine art (discount movie tickets for the unemployed).

Because Perpignan is poor, rents are cheap, and people talk because they haven't much to buy or sell. Because rents are cheap and—this being France—subsidized, old things survive, and idiosyncratic new things, such as circus schools and harmonica clubs, spring up.

Uphill from République is its cut-rate sister, Place Cassanyes, an open market half-Gypsy, half–North African. Here you see every strand of Perpignan Muslim—tall, intensely black Africans in tie-dyed kaftans and leather mules, elderly Arab workingmen in tweed suits and wool watch caps, big-bearded young mullahs in tobacco-colored robes, teenagers in baggies and bandanna head kerchiefs. And Cassanyes leads into the rue Llucia, a humming street jam-packed with storefronts selling date pastries, halal meat, golden slippers, copper braziers, cheap phone calls to Tunisia, Morocco, Algeria, Senegal.

Perhaps because the rue Llucia is so narrow, so bottle-necked by cars whose drivers have stopped to chat with friends, or to dive into a pastry store to pick up lunch, so teeming with customers and goods, because the light is white, the salt sea in the air, you know North Africa is only a ferry ride away. And, curiously, if the rest of Perpignan is a lost-in-time backwater to which *Le Monde* arrives a day late, here in the rue Llucia, you have the feel of a community whose business interests, family ties, and political engagements reach across the Mediterranean to Africa and the Middle East, a community urgently connected to world events, whether the fate of Palestinians, the fallout from September 11th, or the ongoing civil war in Algeria.

Living between two cultures is painful, especially in southern towns like Perpignan with high unemployment and a high quotient of ex-Algerian colonists who want to know why, if the Arabs wanted their own country so badly, they don't stay there. No wonder that certain children of North African immigrants, tired of being second-class citizens, have opted for more uplifting alternative identities. The most tragically famous graduate of Perpignan's best high school, the Lycée Arago, is Zacarias Moussaoui, the born-again son of an adamantly secular Moroccan mother who worked as a cleaning lady for France Telecom. Moussaoui, the accused "twentieth hijacker," who was reported to the FBI for telling his flight teacher he didn't need to learn how to take off or land a 747, now sits in solitary confinement in a Virginia jail, threatened with a death sentence for acts he may or may not have intended to commit.

7

Downtown is where you see the Gypsies on their outings. They are never alone, for a Gypsy alone is like the sole survivor of a horrible accident, bereft and cursed. They are rarely even in pairs, but mostly in great gaggles of eight, nine, ten.

Perpignan is a compact city, and Place de la République is a ten-minute walk from the Gypsy stronghold of St. Jacques. Nonetheless, either because St. Jacques lives are so circumscribed, or because Gypsies fear, with reason, that non-Gypsies despise them, there is often an air of desperate, jailbreak festivity to these group excursions.

The women, pushing baby carriages, cruise the city center, wandering in and out of stores, fingering goods, exclaiming, admiring, depreciating, munching on chocolate bars and drinking cans of Coke they haven't yet bought, shrieking a high Gitan of amusement, scandal, mockery. The mothers, with long hair pulled back by a Spanish comb, tend to look as if they've just gotten out of bed: they wear tight black nylon dresses to the ankle, bedroom slippers. They are often fat, on a scale not common outside the U.S. of A.; this is especially striking in an area where most people are lean.

Obesity is listed as the prime health problem for Perpignan Gypsies of both sexes and all ages. Non-Gypsies are convinced that Perpignan Gypsies blimp on purpose, to get government disability benefits, just as white Americans, in the days before workfare, used to tell you black girls had babies to get more welfare.

The carriages and strollers Gypsy mothers favor are the infantine equivalent of SUVs—superdeluxe and cumbersome chariots bearing children up to five or six years of age. And these children are gargantuanly spoiled. *"Chez les gitans, l'enfant est roi"* is a much-repeated legend, which is truer than the paid-to-be-fat myth, and which reminds you why Americans were so smart to throw out kingship.

One night, coming out of the movies, my husband pointed out to me a little boy of about six, waiting to get into the midnight show of a vampire flick. Not only was he smok-

27

ing a cigarette, but then, having finished it, he stubbed out the butt on his mama's bottom. The mother let out a yelp, but seemed on reflection amused: Gypsy children, especially boys, are *supposed* to act up.

Later on, when my own son, Theodore, would throw a tantrum at being forced to hold a grown-up's hand while crossing a busy street, or kick me hard in the shins for confiscating a carving-knife he fancied, my Gypsy friends would say fondly, approvingly, *"Lui, c'est un vrai gitan."*

The teenaged girls in the women's orbit are a different make from their mothers: tall, still lissome, and decked out in costumes provocative almost to the point of parody—clinging Lurex maxiskirts slit to the thigh, sky-high platform shoes, pharaonic manes of orange-blonde ringlets. But there's a game to the girls' exhibitionism whose rules all the players know: although the skintight skirts appear a blatant invitation, in fact these teenagers are untouchable. Take too long a look, and you're married to her. For what you are witnessing is a perilous interval in which pubescent girls have moved from the license of childhood to the regimen of purity required to ensure an advantageous marriage.

That these fourteen-year-olds might not unequivocally welcome their fate is suggested by the drag-queen edge to their leopard-skin halters and ten-inch heels—gear with a backlash of menace, assumed perhaps not to encourage but to frighten away potential bridegrooms.

The bridegrooms, large gangs of boys ranging in age from twelve to twenty, prowl the same downtown shopping arcades. The little boys are bold, but the young men are timid. They slink, heads bent, cigarettes dripping from downy lips, too poor to stop at cafés, too frightened to look at girls: dark skinny runts, their faces furrowed, scarred, broken, sad.

They are often heartbreakingly beautiful, these boys, sometimes astonishingly debauched-looking, in a manner recalling Caravaggio ephebes, Pasolini's *ragazzi di vita,* and they dress in a bygone style of gangster dandyism. For a start, they wear *suits,* usually white suits with black shirts, or black suits with black shirts. They are loaded with gold: medallions bearing heads of Jesus or Egyptian pharaohs, chunky gold rings, crucifix earrings. They have goatees, sideburns, slicked-back quiffs, they favor octagonal granny glasses tinted yellow, pink, or orange.

Gypsy lives are premodernly short: when boys are five, six years old, their fathers are already throwing them the keys to the car. At thirty, you're middle-aged, at forty, you're a granddaddy. Watching these young men so furtive, so shy on their Saturday afternoon *passegiata,* you have the impression of glimpsing a fragile bloom that will soon burst into sullen jowly maturity.

Once in a blue moon, you see a young man with his wife, pushing the baby carriage, and then there is a sense of infinite weariness, harassment, oppression. They often seemed to be mired in some domestic quarrel you are grateful not to be sharing.

As for the grown men, they don't come downtown. If you want to see them, you must go to St. Jacques's Place Puig or to Place Cassanyes, where—squat, pockmarked, scarred, mustachioed—they sell pajamas, brassieres, triple rolls of sports socks, from a market stall, or play cards in the bar, or hang out in their cars, often an ancient Mercedes or infinitely rehauled Skoda, parked two or three abreast.

Chapter Three

1

Contemporary French has many ways to describe the down-and-out. Politicians and social commentators speak of *"les marginaux," "les défavorisés," "les fragilisés," "les précaires,"* or *"les exclus."* They talk about "the clandestine" or the *"sans-papiers"* (although these last two terms apply to foreigners) and they can refer, with a sympathetic neutrality, to "SDFs" *(sans domicile fixe)*. Visitors to Perpignan are struck by the number of its inhabitants who appear to be all of the above— fragile, out of favor, marginal, precarious, clandestine, and definitely without fixed domicile. This is a place where by a certain time in the month, your friends start to stink, because the electricity that provides their hot water's been cut off.

The sociologist Alain Tarrius, whose specialty is the urban poor, argues in his study of Perpignan that this is a city in which "the margins" are so wide as to constitute, in effect, a new center. Tarrius suggests that it's high time to acknowledge that it is *"we"*—the professional middle classes—who are "the Other," the deviants from an equally valid social, ethical, and economic norm. Recent surveys show that Perpignan has more than twice the national average of unemployment for cities of its size, that more than three times as many of its citizens are on welfare, and that a startling fifty-four percent of the population is engaged in no economic activity whatsoever, although one such study also cautions that true employment is notoriously hard to gauge in a farm economy, where seasonal workers tend to be paid in "black."

Perpignan is the capital of an agricultural province of small farmers whose produce has been undercut by cheaper imports. Roussillon farmers aren't poor, but they maintain an economy fuelled by poor people, a shifting underclass of migrant pickers from as far away as Russia, China, and Ukraine, illegals who squat in condemned buildings in St. Mathieu or around the train station.

I have French friends, too, men and women who pick cherries in the spring, apricots and peaches in the summer, grapes in the fall, sleeping in their cars or in workers' dormitories on-site, and subsisting on unemployment benefits year-round. It's a particular kind of person who likes the rhythm of six weeks' outdoor labor, the brief merry camaraderie of the team, followed by a winter of loafing and odd jobs—house-painting, brick-laying, waitressing, selling bric-a-brac in the markets. Volatile, improvident, hard-drinking, sometimes only one step away from prison or having their children taken away by the state, these are people who when young couldn't sit still at a school desk, and who would rather go hungry than take orders.

On the vineyard on which we live, the workers hired for the *vendange* are for the most part stringy combative men and women, much tattooed, who favor camouflage cutoffs and pit bulls on a leash. Most years, there's a fight, once when the Arabs got tired of racist insults from the "French," again when a boy who had been advanced his season's wages got thirsty and decided he'd been cheated.

In his history of the Mediterranean in the sixteenth century, Fernand Braudel describes much the same crew seasonally descending upon this littoral plain: a "procession . . . of landless peasants, unemployed artisans, casual agricultural workers down for the harvest, the *vendange,* or the threshing, outcasts of society, beggars and beggar-women, travelling preachers, *gyrovaques,* street musicians, and shepherds with their flocks."

In Roussillon, you can still see all of these, including preachers and shepherds. But it's the preponderance of Braudel's seasonal drifters, odd-jobbers, and roustabouts that give downtown Perpignan its raffishness, a hint of vagabond festivity that is quick to turn to menace. I have never been anywhere, including New York's Bowery in the 1970s, where you see more black eyes, and yet this is also a city in which a stolen car or a break-in is mostly as bad as crime gets, and where local libertarians went haywire when the police installed video surveillance in St. Mathieu in order to crack down on drug-dealing.

A girl I know asked a homeless Scottish ex-legionnaire she'd befriended why there were so many tramps in Perpignan. He told her that homeless people across Europe spread the word that Perpignan is a safe haven, and that street people who've met in Berlin or Seville gather every spring for a reunion. I am not sure if he wasn't pulling her leg, but it's true that every spring, Roussillon sees the return not only of flamingoes, nightingales, and hoopoes, but also great congregations of plum-faced young tramps, drinking on the steps of the market-square theater, washing their clothes and watering their dogs in the fountain by the Promenade des Platanes.

2

On one of the highest hills of Perpignan sits St. Jacques, known in Gitan as San Jaume. St. Jacques has long been home to undesirables. In the Middle Ages, it was a leper colony. Then it became the Jewish *Call,* whose gates were locked at night. When Jews were expelled from Spanish Roussillon in 1493, St. Jacques's synagogue and *mikvah* were quarried to build new monasteries on the same sites, including one specifically for converted Jews. In an exhibition on Perpignan Jews, I saw a letter from Ferdinand II revoking—in response to complaints from the Dominican convent—his earlier edict which made the *Call* the official residence of Perpignan's prostitutes. By the Second World War, St. Jacques was once again a poor Jewish quarter. With the fall of France, there was a quick shuffle in which Jews forced to flee sold their houses to Gypsies forced to settle.

A Gypsy patriarch interviewed by Alain Tarrius recalls three Pétain officials searching his house in August 1942 for its former Jewish owners. One of the men spat in his face, telling him, " 'We prefer cholera to the plague. When there's no more plague, when you have helped us to kill them all, then we'll take care of the cholera: that's when I'll be back to see you.' We were the cholera and the Jews were the plague," he recounts.

At the summit of St. Jacques is Place Puig, dominated by the Caserne, a vast, early-nineteenth-century ochre-stucco army garrison with green shutters, which during the war was used to intern Gypsies (the overflow was sent to the Rivesaltes camp) and in the '70s was finally renovated into permanent government housing. Today, the Caserne's got the reputation of being a fundamentalist redoubt of hard-core Gypsydom: the Wild West, says Diane, firing off imaginary bullets from her cocked fingers. From miles away, you can spot the Caserne looming above St. Jacques, half-macabre, half-jaunty, like a prison ship in which the inmates have seized command.

From the Place Puig, narrow streets run steeply downhill through a headlong warren of decrepit houses, where empty window frames are covered in plastic sheeting and hammered sides of olive-oil cans, and front doors, chalked with the names of their inhabitants, are fastened with a loop of rope. Sanitation in St. Jacques is intermittent: you see girls filling plastic tankards from the cast-iron pump in the Place Puig.

One icy-blue winter's day, I toured St. Jacques with a Frenchman called Stéphane Henri. Stéphane Henri is a short, solid-packed ex-Parisian with a long, grizzled black ponytail and a round, twinkly face like a hedgehog. Today, fighting a head cold, he's wearing several layers of brightly colored sweaters and carrying a packet of Fisherman's Friend cough drops and a bag of lemons. Stéphane Henri, despite his confessed anarchist sympathies, works for the Ministry of Education. His job is making French public schools more congenial to Gypsy children. As he takes me though the nursery and primary schools of St. Jacques, he explains to me some of the problems he faces.

"The French Republican system was designed to make people docile for factory jobs. It's too rigid to accommodate Gypsies—to acknowledge, for example, that when these children arrive in the classroom, they have never even *heard* French, except on television. So far, we've got an okay pre-school system, but when the real learning begins, they bomb out. And nobody, *nobody* continues school past fourteen."

"Why not?"

"Well, what's the point? Traditionally, the Gypsies of Roussillon were horse-breeders, blacksmiths, basket-weavers. They traveled the markets, buying and selling. By the '60s, their trades had become obsolete. The old social contract of finish your education and you'll get a good job no longer applies. Now they live off welfare, and there are no jobs anyway."

It's even worse for the girls, Stéphane Henri continues; they get yanked out of school as soon as they hit puberty. "Because most high schools are coed, fathers are scared that if their daughter's seen hanging out with boys, she'll ruin her reputation and won't be able to make a good marriage.

"It's my impression that the marriage age in St. Jacques is actually dropping. Girls who ten, twenty years ago would have gotten married at eighteen are now being married off at fifteen, before they have a chance to make a *connerie.*' A pediatrician friend of mine with a clinic at Place Cassanyes, tells me of seeing a new mother so young she stayed playing with the LEGOs in the waiting room while the grandmother brought the baby in for its examination.

We pass a knot of older men in black suits and white shirts, who turn around to look at us. These men, Stéphane Henri explains, are pastors of the Pentacostalist Church.

In the early '60s, Roussillon Gypsies plying the markets of northern France encountered Protestant evangelism. Many young men got converted and were reborn as Penta-costalist preachers—a brand of clergyman that was appealing to former Catholics because it required neither study nor celibacy, but only native eloquence. Today, the evangelical *Assemblées* are what remain in Gypsy Perpignan as a governing authority. The Gypsies of St. Jacques have no more kings, but they have pastors. There are few cafés or groceries or businesses in St. Jacques, but instead there are shabby storefronts labeled in red paint HOLY RADIANCE or LIGHT AND LIFE, where on weekday nights you find a room packed with twenty-year-olds singing gospel songs testifying to Jesus's loving grace.

Pentacostalism, to Stéphane Henri's mind, has been a great force of reaction. "Those pastors are terrible frauds: they say to us, Yes, yes, children must stay in school, but what they preach is that the Internet is the devil, and that Gypsy society is falling apart because husbands are letting their wives run around the streets."

3

What I really want to ask Stéphane Henri about is the problem of Gypsy vote-buying. For much of the last four decades, Perpignan has been ruled by the Alduy family. In 1959, Paul Alduy quit his job as mayor of a nearby spa town (his wife Jacqueline took over) and became the mayor of Perpignan, and in 1993, their son Jean-Paul succeeded him.

Paul Alduy applied to this medieval Mediterranean jewel the postwar American model of urban planning: let the inner city rot, quarantine it with a beltway, and beyond, suburban housing for middle-class commuters. Paul Alduy plunked a multistory parking lot in the middle of Perpignan's ancient market square, and ran highways through the lovely Roman-

esque villages outlying Perpignan, drowning them in contin-
uous suburb.

Jean-Paul Alduy, the current mayor, is a different character. He is an ex-Trotskyist intellectual whose wife is the man-
aging director of *Le Monde*. He got his degree in urban
planning from one of France's distinguished *grandes écoles*,
and he is clearly in love with the heady brew of old-fashioned
elegance and raunchiness, the polyglot civilities—and jeering,
brazen incivilities—that make up an old Mediterranean city.
Paul Alduy lived in one of the suburbs he himself had developed. Jean-Paul lives in an old *hotel particulier* downtown.

The changes Alduy junior has made to Perpignan's
urban fabric are both small and choice. He's repaved cement
sidewalks in the local red-and-white-veined marble; he's renovated tumbledown houses in St. Jacques or St. Mathieu, one
by one, and beautifully—the way you would if you wanted
to live there yourself; he's banned cars from the canal-side
Quai Vauban, where Perpignanais take their Saturday afternoon promenade, and replanted it with plane trees. Most sig-
nificantly, he's spending millions to bury underground the
multistory parking lot with which his father defaced Place de
la République. It's proof of Jean-Paul Alduy's catholic sympathies that when I ask to meet the founder of the Mediator,
the hip downtown venue where you go to hear the best
international jazz, salsa, techno, hip-hop, I am asked, "You
mean the mayor?"

But the underside to Mediterranean tolerance is clien-
telism. It was Alduy's father who realized thirty years ago
that he could consistently win reelection by turning St.
Jacques and the outlying Gypsy neighborhood of Haut Vernet into rotten boroughs, under the rule of a party stalwart
entrusted with buying the Gypsy vote. Under Alduy senior,

according to a report in *L'Express,* the ward boss of St. Jacques used to hand out banknotes in broad daylight just before election day. Today, it's Alduy junior's official Gypsy "mediators" who allegedly distribute apartments, disability benefits, and no-show jobs in exchange for votes.

The goodies can be pretty comic. Perpignanaises love to tell you how, just before the 1995 elections, St. Jacques was flooded in scooters: suddenly every boy in the neighborhood was zooming around on a Solex that was a present from Uncle Mayor, a reminder to the kid's parents to be *sage* on election day.

"Haven't you heard the story?" asks a friend from the rival Gypsy neighborhood of Haut Vernet, in disgust. "They weren't even nice new scooters. The *conseiller général* had a friend who owned a motorbike-rental shop at Canet Plage. At the end of a couple of seasons, he has fifty used scooters, it's time to buy newer models, so he unloads them in St. Jacques, in exchange for who knows what dirty favor. Here in Haut Vernet, we have only beat-up stolen scooters: here we are given apartments instead."

When I ask Stéphane Henri about the Alduy family's electoral use of Gypsies, he shakes his head. "Ten, fifteen years ago, there was still one ruling patriarch of St. Jacques. Now there isn't. But there are clans, and the mayor has encouraged rivalries, tensions among the clans by favoring some over others. 'Divide and conquer.'

"The worst of all is that the mayor has picked harmless old men who otherwise would be doddering grandfathers, and enthroned them as 'mediators,' with the power to hand out favors. It's retrograde, and it further disempowers women.

"Until last year, the ward boss of St. Jacques was Henri

Carbonell, a funeral-home owner who was also deputy mayor," Stéphane Henri continues, lowering his voice as we pass two Gypsies wearing the fluorescent green uniforms of garbagemen, a job that in St. Jacques is a government sinecure. "Carbonell got fired for being too blatant in his vote-buying, so now in the good old fascist style, it's his wife Madeleine who's taken his place. This year it's not scooters or refrigerators, it's jobs and apartments."

I remember the Gypsy patriarch, quoted by Alain Tarrius, who described the Pétainist officials who searched his house for Jews and spat in his face, warning, "When there's no more plague, we'll be back to take care of the cholera." The old man went on to say, "I've never been too reassured by those *paios* who have come to visit us before every election since the '70s, because I recognize exactly the same faces I saw that day in August 1942. They've kept the same people who've always worked for them—for them, or for their fathers."

Stéphane Henri takes me past a nursery school. We peek through the window into a room full of toddlers, who are hanging close to the long black skirts of women whom I take to be their mothers, but whom he explains are teachers.

"Don't let them see you," Stéphane Henri warns, but it is too late. A little girl, catching sight of us, bursts out howling, and races across the room to hide in a teacher's lap. Afterward, he explains, "There's always at least one who starts bawling at the sight of a *paio*."

At the end of the day, I ask Stéphane Henri what his ideal is for children growing up in St. Jacques today. "Gypsy modernity," he replies. "Not assimilation—modernity. That the kids I work with grow up into happy outgoing people with real jobs that aren't just government bribes. The only hope is the women, who are more progressive. Their lives are already shit, so they've got nothing to lose."

<h1 style="text-align:center">4</h1>

In the early 1990s, a plague struck St. Jacques.

For a decade or so, Gypsy men had been in the habit of buying heroin on their trips to Barcelona. They would pick up a couple of grams in the Barrio Chino, and bring them back to Perpignan for themselves and their families. Heroin addiction spread through the neighborhood, followed by AIDS.

French people who don't like Gypsies look at the big cars that trawl through St. Jacques and say, Drug money. But in fact, most of those cars, usually a mustard-yellow or pistachio-green Mercedes, are twenty years old, have engines cannibalized from much cheaper cars, and were bought in Bulgaria for less than you would pay for a new Peugeot 306.

Alain Tarrius spent a couple of years in the '90s researching Perpignan Gypsies and their drug use—research which included such unusual methods as himself passing drugs between Barcelona dealers—and concluded that the Catalan Gypsies of St. Jacques were not sellers, but small-time consumers who bought just enough "for the family." Unfortunately, the collective nature of Gypsy life made the spread of AIDS in St. Jacques particularly uncontrollable. St. Jacques's heroin users were not ones to sneak off to the bathroom at parties. Instead, the men sat round the kitchen table and passed the needle from uncle to nephew to cousin to grandfather, much as they might pass a guitar. (Women were not allowed to touch the goods.) Which meant that entire clans were getting infected, that several generations of women were losing fathers, husbands, sons—first to the addiction, then to the disease. Gypsy attitudes toward sickness and death made treatment tricky. Jews responded to the Holocaust by making sure nobody would ever forget; Gypsies, who call it the Swallowing-Up, with rare exceptions don't want to know.

Lamia Missaoui, a Perpignan sociologist who wrote a book called *Gitans et Santé de Barcelone à Turin,* chronicled St. Jacques clans in which uncles were HIV-positive and brothers had fullblown AIDS, but other family members who had shared needles refused to be tested, and those with HIV wouldn't follow through with treatment. If you don't look at it, it goes away.

There were alarmist figures in local newspapers: otherwise rational French people still tell you with absolute assurance that as much as eighty percent of the adult male Gypsy population of Perpignan is HIV-positive. People predicted extermination: in twenty years, there would be no more Gypsies in St. Jacques. Nobody seemed too sad.

But somehow, drug users pulled back from the brink, and the epidemic has peaked. The dying died, but nobody new got sick. Former junkies were reborn as evangelical preachers, one mother who had lost her son to AIDS founded the Women in Black protest movement, and the disease never made that crossover to women and their babies that has cursed other parts of the world.

Teenagers tell you, "I saw my uncle turn to a vegetable; I don't want to go that way."

5

If it were only a question of AIDS-infected junkies and little boys with a predilection for stubbing out their cigarettes on their mothers' bottoms, you might wonder why I was so keen to get to know Perpignan Gypsies. Most other people in Perpignan, after all, do their damnedest *not* to meet Gypsies.

But what I had discovered was that this small city, thanks to its Gypsies, has long been a musical mecca: home to a brand of music called Gypsy rumba that, in the hands of its keenest practitioners, gives you goose bumps. My introduction to Gypsy rumba was a joyous shock. One night, I went to the Mediator to hear a Colombian swing band. Opening for them was a group called Rumba Mayor.

Six boys filed onto the stage. They were beautiful boys, startlingly young—the youngest not yet fourteen, and almost catatonic with stage fright. Five of the boys were Gypsies, dressed in black suits and white shirts, golden crucifixes. They looked like child preachers who might be about to speak in tongues or handle snakes. The sixth boy was Arab— a bright-burning spark of nervous energy, who wore a rough, homespun hooded djellabah.

These were street kids from St. Jacques. Their instruments were minimal—guitars, *cajon* (a wooden percussion box, on which the player sits). But when the chubby, red-cheeked lead singer, Jean Ramon, unleashed a husky wail in counterpoint to Majid's nasal Arabic lament, there was a catch between the racy lolloping beat and the sad song that grabbed your heart. You were hearing a band that was barely born, still wet behind the ears, half-somber, half-exultant with newness. Yet these musicians seemed already to possess a preternatural restraint, an intuitive understanding of how to reap powerful effect from slender means. That night, when the six boys sat in a semicircle and, without voices or instruments, launched into a suite of brisk, intricately syncopated hand-clapping—a flamenco technique known as *palmas*—it was thrilling. These were teenaged musicians who weren't afraid of quiet, even silence.

6

For forty years, the Catalan Gypsy clans of this region have been producing great bands, several of whom have gone on to achieve international fame. In the '70s, it was Manitas del Plata, in the '80s, the Gipsy Kings.

The music that's come out of this Franco-Spanish borderland is born of *"Ida y Vuelta"* (Coming and Going)— the transatlantic crisscrossings by which Yoruban music brought by African slaves to the New World produced a Latin American/Caribbean fusion, which Spanish sailors then brought back to Mediterranean ports. There, Gypsies adapted this new music to their own ends, using the necks of their guitars and the palms of their hands instead of the conga drums and calabashes of Afro-Latin music.

In the 1960s, as Catalan Gypsies were evangelized by the Pentacostalists, this music was "born again" too, so that much of what I took at first to be love songs in fact were gospel hymns. The blend of loony upbeat Afro-Caribbean bounce and hoarse flamenco-style yowls of brokenhearted prayer—an effect as schizophrenically original as R & B— created a music that seemed to express the perverse vagaries of a soul yearning for union with God.

After that first snatch of Rumba Mayor, I was lost. From then on, my afternoons were spent leafing through second-hand record stores in search of *tanguillos* played by Els Rumberos Catalans de Sant Jaume or a fandango by Josep "El Chabo" Vila, former guitarist for Manitas del Plata, my evenings at the festivals which give southern towns an air of semipermanent carnival, at which you could hear the newest Gypsy bands alongside local hip-hop or reggae groups.

Because this is Republican France, where even the ruling right-of-center believes that subsidized culture is a form of nationalism (not to mention that kids who play the guitar are less likely to be stealing car radios), these teen guttersnipes would often be performing in the most exquisite sites: in deconsecrated medieval monasteries or in the Catalan Gothic patio of the Palais des Rois de Majorque.

But going to a Gypsy concert in Perpignan, I discovered, was a different experience either from hearing local "French" groups or from hearing Gypsy music in other towns. When you went to hear Els Rumberos Catalans in Toulouse, say, the audience, predominately student, would shout the encouragements common to Spanish Gypsy music—*"Hombre!"* and *"Gitano!"*—whooping, ululating, warmheartedly pounding for encores. If you heard the same band in Perpignan, however, there were few "French" people in the audience. The crowd would be predominately fat mothers in black, pushing baby carriages. There would be knots of young preacher types, knots of girls in maxiskirts accompanied by their chaperones, and two dozen little boys swirling across the dance floor or the open square.

The atmosphere would be less concert than country fair, where adepts looking over the horses know better than to drive up the price by any display of undue interest. Although the audience was one hundred percent familial, nobody applauded, nobody cheered. It seemed a code of honor not to act impressed. In Gypsy music, I learned, there is always the attitude, You think he's something? You should have heard his grandmother. There is an ambivalence toward fame, a tradition of performers who don't like to perform—especially not before non-Gypsies—an ethic of dynastic amateurism, where the best musicians are the oldest, the ones who only sang over the kitchen table. To me, a product of American youth culture, it was touching that David Argeles, the guitarist of Rumba Mayor, was so young that when he sat down to play, his feet didn't reach the ground. But to those who knew better, he was an ignorant upstart.

After one concert at the Mediator, a hunched, wizened, Neanderthal-looking man in a dirty jean jacket was dragged from the crowd, hoisted onstage, and cajoled into singing. The voice that came out of him was huge: a primal wail with a vibrato powerful as an ocean liner's foghorn. And this time, the audience clapped and cheered. I asked everybody who he was, and several months later I found out. He was the uncle of one of the musicians playing that night, I was told. The fall guy in a drug bust, he had spent his adult life in a Barcelona jail, and only just been sprung.

7

I learned most of what I know about Gypsy groups playing rumba from an Irishman named Garth.

Garth is the only person I've met for whom Gypsies profess unanimous affection. He works at the Casa Musicale, on the edge of St. Jacques. The Casa is a walled compound enclosing both the old arsenal belonging to the still functioning garrison across the street, and also the ruined Couvent des Grands Carmes, a fourteenth-century monastery whose surviving church was burned down at the end of the Second World War. Its massive stone structure, grassy, roofless, is now used for sculptors' installations. In the '90s, this ruined religious-military compound was acquired by the government and converted into a neighborhood arts center. This is where kids come to study blues guitar or *cajon,* where they form bands, rehearse, perform in the newly renovated theater, record their own demos, and play in the Casa's summer festival, alongside more established international groups.

The Casa is the brain-child of Guy Bertrand, a clarinetist who was professor of traditional music at Perpignan's conservatory in the '80s and '90s, and who singlehandedly brought about the revival of Gypsy music in Perpignan. Guy Bertrand has since been promoted to the conservatory of Lyons, and today the animating force behind Gypsy music at the Casa is his brother-in-law, Garth Beattie.

One night in pouring rain, I went to visit Garth, a ropy, freckled redhead in his mid-50s. He is a farm boy from Northern Ireland; his only brother was a soldier in the British Army. He's had a vagabond life. He worked at the jazz club Ronnie Scott's in London, he tells me, he cooked and babysat for the American expatriate artist R. J. Kitaj, he worked for a Harvard doctor who treated the mentally ill, and for a video-maker in the Colorado desert. Now he lives in Espira del Agly, a Catalan wine-making village outside Perpignan, with his wife, Pascale, who teaches high school and is Guy Bertrand's sister, and their little girl, Juliette. He's a practiced raconteur, merry, stoical, and you know that whatever wild thing you might have done in your youth, he's done two times over.

We sit in the Portakabin that is Garth's office, drinking tea, and Garth introduces me to Josep, Fabien, Chris, Jean Ramon, Majid, and Pips. The musicians I have been hearing in concert materialize into glum shy homebodies who like to sit, arms wrapped tight around each others' necks.

Garth treats these young men with a sardonic scolding affection permanently on the verge of explosive frustration. Teasing covers outright despair. If you didn't laugh, his stories suggest, you'd get to despise St. Jacques musicians. His brother-in-law, Guy Bertrand, who "invented" Perpignan Gypsy music and who continues to manage and produce the best bands, has come to despise them. But Guy Bertrand was expecting that the Gypsy musicians he managed would learn to work as hard at their own music as he did. Garth, although he may once have had higher hopes, now appears content just to be loved by these slum kids and their families.

French people pronounce Garth's name "Garce." *"Garce"* in French is slang for "whore." Gypsies prefer to call him Johnny, and they say it with a proprietary tenderness. The guitarist Jeannot Soler—a bitter character not normally given to sentimentality—tells me, hand on his heart, "Johnny is the best friend I have in the world. He has a heart of gold. You can't imagine the effect of Johnny—this redhead, hand in hand with his little daughter, strolling through St. Jacques in deepest winter in a pair of shorts and a tank-top—People's minds are blown."

From time to time, I visit Garth in his Portakabin office that's icy in winter, sweltering in summer. We sit with his colleague, Joseph Poubil, a sweet, beaky-nosed young *cajon*-player who is the only Gypsy I meet in Roussillon who shows up every day to an office job. We drink tea, we chat with the musicians who drop by, we exchange favorite tapes. And Garth tries to explain to me about Gypsy musicians in St. Jacques.

"Having worked with the mentally retarded, I'm well placed!" he jokes.

It's often a story of defeat. "Most of these bands fall apart, because they're lazy." Even the glorious Rumba Mayor has just broken up, to everybody's sorrow. One problem, Garth maintains, is that Gypsies start too young. "These kids can make music when they're six or seven years old, they can even form a band, but they've never had any training, and they're *limited*. It's harder to 'unlearn' and start from scratch when you've been strumming on a guitar or banging on drums since you were born.

"In Seattle, kids will practice in a freezing garage every night all winter, and after three years they're Nirvana. Here, the French state gives them whatever they need—except motivation.

"A band gets invited to a festival, and they don't want to go. Why not? Well, the great irony of Gypsies here is they're scared to travel! So you take them to this festival, which is run on a shoestring, and they think they should get paid half a million dollars. So they complain about the accommodations, and they throw the food on the floor, because it's not their kind of food, and they start grumbling about *paios,* and that's when I try to explain to them that *paios* is a silly idea that's beside the point, that these are people who are trying to give them a break."

"I took NG San Jaume to play a festival in Poitiers. It was their first out-of-town gig: they were excited, they were a hit, but after they came back, they didn't show up to practice for six weeks. You ask why—well, the family had to celebrate their return. It's not easy to work with Gypsies, they definitely have a different sense of priorities."

It's Saturday lunch at Garth and Pascale's house in Espira. "It's an endless racket," Pascale, a small, animated woman, confirms. "After so many years together, these Gypsies are still ripping you off at every corner: I won't play tonight if you don't give me this, buy me that, pay me that." One night on tour, they discovered the lead guitarist couldn't play because he'd just sold the strings off his guitar.

"Their sense of reality is not very strong." She recalls a singer calling her up two days *after* his band had left for Australia, explaining he hadn't been able to make the flight, but maybe he could go next week instead, and that he was planning to bring along a friend because he didn't want to fly alone.

"Well," says Pascale, "how do you begin explaining to a grown man that actually, no, if he missed his flight, he missed it, and since the ticket to Australia he's just pissed away cost a thousand dollars at a *discount,* no, he *cannot* bring along a date."

I myself witness the drummer Chris Mailly, a gentle, charming, nineteen-year-old from Rumba Mayor, being invited to join a reggae band that's going on a world tour. Chris mutters a gloomy assent.

The Parisian producer, thinking Chris must have misunderstood, repeats his proposition. You, Chris, having learned to play reggae drums and sing English lyrics—"I don't think that will be possible," Chris interjects, soberly—will cut a CD. We will then go on tour *to Africa.* Pause. *The Caribbean.* Pause, while Yves waits for a reaction. Get it? Palm trees, piña coladas, girls in string bikinis? *America.* *"D'accord?"*

Chris *is* reacting: it's just that he's reacting as if he's been told his mother has cancer. He sighs a near groan, monumentally depressed.

"Give me your telephone number," says Yves.

"I don't have a telephone."

"Your cell phone?"

"I don't have one."

"Your beeper number?"

No beeper.

"What if someone wants to get hold of you?"

Unintelligible mumble.

"Here. Here is *my* number," says Yves, the first note of sarcasm creeping into his showman's brightness. "Do you think you could find your way to a telephone booth to call me?"

Wretched nod.

Only by the end of the evening, romping in NG San Jaume's rehearsal room, mussing Fabien's hair, chewing on Pips's earring, has Chris recovered his high spirits, the horrible opportunity quite forgotten.

But as Garth tells it, amid the frustrations of trying to get Gypsies out of their rut, there are moments of redemption. Ecstatic all-nighters, such as the impromptu celebration of a Hungarian musician's birthday in Sydney, when Gypsies from Romania, Rajasthan, South America, and St. Jacques passed the guitar from hand to hand.

To me, Gypsies have always been the exotic Other. But what I realize, talking to Garth and his associates, is that to them, St. Jacques Gypsies are the opposite of exotic: they are ignorant shut-ins who desperately need to be coaxed out of their rut. When Garth speaks of getting St. Jacques musicians to jam with Tzigane groups from the Balkans, his eyes light up in much the same way as do those of a social worker

I meet who describes the delight of taking Gypsy mothers up into the mountains for a day's sledding: women who from the windows of their project can see the icy slopes of Canigou, the highest mountain in the Mediterranean Pyrenees, but who have never in their lives touched snow.

Chapter Four

1

The first rainy winter night I visited Garth in his Portakabin, he sent me away with a book and a handful of CDs. I had heard all the newest rumba bands in St. Jacques, and we were rooting for the same teams, but Garth wanted to give me a sense of the larger context in which this music belonged. The CDs were recordings of some of the great Spanish flamenco artists—both legends from the 1930s and contemporary innovators such as Tomatito and José Mercé, who were renewing the tradition from within.

"You can't understand St. Jacques without knowing flamenco," was Garth's message.

The book he lent me was by a Frenchman called Bernard Leblon who has spent the past forty years living with the Franco-Spanish Gypsies of Roussillon. This particular book was a study of flamenco.

Flamenco today is a subject that attracts musicologists worldwide: there are yearly conferences and competitions, music labels that produce antiquarian field recordings, numerous theories as to whether it's Spanish Gypsies' Indo-

Iranian origins or Spain's long Arab-Jewish centuries that makes this music of Gypsy Spain so "Oriental" in its beats, melodies, and vocal range. All we know for sure is that the Gypsies who came into Spain via Roussillon in the 1400s effected a Nietzschean "transvaluation of values."

Whereas, according to Bernard Leblon, popular Spanish singers favored sweetness and clarity of tone, Gypsy musicians introduced what's called in Romany *loki djili* (long song) and in Andalusian *cante jondo* (deep song), a music characterized by silences and breaks within a word or couplet, startling shifts of rhythm, trance-like repetitions of nonsense sounds, whines, howls, groans, wails, and weird trills and vibrati, along with background encouragement of the lead singer from other musicians rather like a gospel meeting's "Hallelujah," or "Say it like it is, sister."

"Flamenco is our blues," the musician Joseph Poubil explains to me. When someone compares a brand of music to the American blues, he's telling you it's poor people's music that takes place in a world of manual labor (the slowest, heaviest rhythm in flamenco is called *martinete* after the blacksmith's hammer), sickness, debt, jail (there's an entire category of prison songs called *carcelera*), alcohol, and God.

In flamenco, old and broken is better than new. The virtues prized in the classical Western tradition, Bernard Leblon explains, in flamenco are considered defects. Instead, there is "an aesthetic of ruin which praises aged artists," a "cult of amusicality," "a counter-aesthetic of paroxysm and suffering," of "hoarse, broken, croaking nasal voices, tarred by the Gypsy smithy." "To be really great, you have to be really horrible. You don't say a singer has a beautiful voice, but *'una voz que hiere,'* a voice that wounds."

In Franco's Spain, flamenco became a countercultural force revered by anti-fascist intellectuals. Bernard Leblon has a theory that flamenco got "reorientalized" during such periods of Gypsy persecution, when singers no longer had to appeal to a popular taste for bel canto, but could howl and moan and croak as they chose, naked voices accompanied only by the palms of their hands.

Listening to CDs of Perpignan rumba artists, I had noticed that the accompanying texts invariably mentioned the musicians' lineage: the four Saadna brothers had been taught to play by their maternal uncles, the flamenco master Chele and the rumba king Luis Giminez. The father of the three Espinas brothers was a composer of Pentacostalist hymns; their maternal uncles were likewise precocious adepts of the Barcelona rumba. The longevity of some of these bands was impressive. I ask Garth what it means that Els Rumberos Catalans—men still in their forties—have been performing nearly thirty years. "What's it mean?" he says, drily. "It means they're brothers, that's what it means."

For Andalusian flamenco artists, too, family appeared inescapable. The profession was ruled by musical dynasties, several of them reaching back to the eighteenth century, and each with its own house style.

This family-mindedness, this respect for lineage and tradition, this habit of deferring to elders, which characterizes both flamenco and St. Jacques rumba, encourages an ethic of anti-professionalism and of anti-individualism even, a cult of the unrecorded amateur which is miles away from They-must-be-good-because-they-got-signed-by-a-major-record-label-and-made-the-cover-of-*Rolling-Stone*.

Among flamenco artists, there is a belief that music is in the blood and hence cannot really be taught, that it is a spirit that cannot be summoned at will, but only comes when it pleases. When you are seized by the mood, you enter a Sufic trance, a state of total abandon. (Bernard Leblon writes of flamenco artists who play for twenty-four hours at a go.) When the audience is all wrong, the ambience cold, you find yourself mute, impotent. Cunning artists, however, find ways to slip the bridle over their muse's head.

Leblon quotes the writer Federico Garcia Lorca's description of how the great Nina de los Peines, in a Cádiz bar, unable to move "an audience of stone," grabs a glass of eau-de-vie and downs it in one gulp. Only then, once she'd burned her throat raw and lost her breath, "bankrupt[ed] her native gifts and dismiss[ed] her surest techniques," could she find her voice.

I myself witnessed a similarly Dionysian descent one night at the Theâtre de la République in Perpignan. The guitarist Pedro Soler had had the bright idea of bringing together two of his favorite divas—the flamenco singer Ines Bacan and the Arab-Andalusian singer Amina Alaoui. The evening felt like a Middle East peace conference. Each woman sang in turn, accompanied on guitar or oud by her own courtier, refusing to acknowledge the other's presence, and the audience was made up of constipated Catalans come out for an evening of intercommunal understanding, who had been too well taught as children that the proper way to behave in a theater is to sit still.

Ines Bacan, a hefty alto, grew increasingly red-faced and desperate. Finally, making a bow, she tripped on her stiletto heel, toppled over the edge of the stage, and in hideous slow-motion, fell into the audience.

I think Ines Bacan willed herself to fall. Because it required just such a sacrifice—such a comic catastrophe, when everyone present had to swallow the terrified compulsion to laugh—in order to win over her audience and cosinger. And having "fallen," Ines Bacan herself was shocked back into her voice.

Flamenco, I was getting the impression, is the art of desperate measures, the winning of a fugitive grace from failure, bankruptcy, shame. It's this spirit of sly abasement, of antinomian reversals and tear-soaked triumphs that makes it so inherently religious.

I was hearing good musicians in Perpignan who had remained true to flamenco's purest origins and impulses. There was Olivier Martinez, aka Kanélé, a young Andalusian Gypsy singer who was venturing deep into the heart of rhythm and who—in an otherwise all "French" *cuadro*, including a violinist and a dancer—was painstakingly, solitarily working out something new. There was the lamentedly short-lived Rumba Mayor, who had had the brilliant idea of merging Gypsy rumba and Algerian *rai* in a fusion that was completely local and authentic. But there was one Perpignan band that was so superlative, so God-graced, that it just wasn't fair, that you held your breath while you listened, and remembered what voices and hands were made for. This was Moïse's Tekameli. This book is an homage to Tekameli—to all that Tekameli could be, and all that they will never become. Because they are Perpignan Gypsies, and would rather play gin rummy all day in a fairground bar than rehearse, would rather stay home with their families than pursue fame in the foreign capitals of world music.

Imagine a CD, as cut on the eve of the second millennium. A CD is a cultic vessel, ultraslim, microcondensed, encoding image, text, sound on a winged silver wafer.

It is a portable shrine. In the old days, when people journeyed, they took with them their household gods. Remember Rachel snitching her father's idols when she and Jacob set off on their travels? Today we grab a handful of CDs—for luck, for consolation, for private consumption, as a declaration of identity and allegiance in alien surroundings.

Who are you? the sailors ask Jonah as the ship is sinking. What is your occupation? Where do you come from? What is your country, and of what people are you?

Questions not so different from what we find today on customs declarations.

I am a Hebrew, and I fear the Lord, the God of Heaven. Who are you?

I am an American, and I listen to Radiohead, Nine Inch Nails, and Death in Vegas.

Ida y Vuelta is a supremely cultic CD. It was produced in 1999 by Sony, one of the biggest worldwide media conglomerates, and it features a band called Tekameli.

But this particular offering of Sony's is veiled, hermetic. The group is unknown, their name is impenetrable, and the album's Spanish title is a cipher (who's Ida?). The musical tradition and ethnographic context they come from—explained with maps and diagrams on an inside flap—are equally arcane. Add to the confusion that the musicians are Frenchmen singing Pentacostalist hymns in a language—Gypsy Catalan—that very few people know exists. It brings news from a place no one's heard of, and the news is at once too close and too distant to be intelligible.

2

I bought my CD of *Ida y Vuelta* at Lolita Disques.

Perpignan is probably the only French city of over 100,000 that doesn't have an outlet of the music-and-book chain Fnac. For years, Mayor Alduy has been trying to coax Fnac into opening a branch in a boarded-up Belle Epoque palace that was formerly a women's department store. If Fnac does deem it worthwhile to establish an outpost in Perpignan, the city center may no longer be quite so shuttered closed and empty by nightfall, but it will probably mean death to the dozens of secondhand bookstores and cult vinyl shops that flourish here in the absence of multinationals.

Lolita is a tiny record store on the market square of République, hidden by fruit-and-vegetable stalls, and run by three crewcut music fanatics, who also act as DJs for evenings of their favorite music at local nightspots. One of them, Jeff, is a Catalan who lived the punk years in Notting Hill; he spends a month a year in India and likes to discuss the effect of the Algerian war of independence on the contemporary French psyche. Jeff's got his own musical obsessions, but he knows my tastes, and is determined to improve them. Every time I come in, he gives me a tip, or throws in a freebie. "Here, listen to them."

When I ask him about Tekameli, he shrugs. Of course they're the best, he himself lives on the edge of St. Jacques and is among the very few Catalans who get along with Gypsies, but being St. Jacques Gypsies, Tekameli's going to blow the chance offered by its Sony deal.

"Did you hear their last concert at the Mediator, where they tried to sound like hard rock? It was completely *nul*."

Other Franco-Spanish Gypsy groups have catchy accessible names: the Gipsy Kings, El Principe Gitano, El Rumberos. "Tekameli" is a word from Kalo, the Spanish dialect of Romany of which present-day Gitan retains only stray words. "Tekameli," which was suggested to the group by their pastor, means "I love you." ("You," I imagine, is not some girl, but Jesus.) The name is theirs—secret, a come-and-find-me tease.

And the photographs in the CD's folder are equally defi-ant: a family album of Roussillon Gypsydom, a guided tour to the trashy-forlorn joys of this forgotten bordertown's slums, its beach resorts, its scrubland.

On the cover, bathed in golden light, the musicians clus-ter below the Ferris wheel of the yearly funfair staged on the banks of the river Tet—a sweet, raucous funfair, whose rifle ranges and coconut tosses operate on the principle that all players should win a prize, every time, and from which you come home groaning with goldfish, tattoo kits, and Indian bows and arrows.

Inside, the musicians are at their favorite pastimes: pic-tures as emblematic for posterity as Roman tombs on which the cobbler is shown with his awl.

Salomon holds a white horse by the bridle.

Moïse, his brother, on a ruined street in St. Jacques, cups between his hands the golden-white whirr of a fighting cock's feathers and spurs.

Jeannot, a skinny alley cat, leans against the stripped car-cass of a Deux Chevaux in a salvage yard.

Tato, the family man, is shown on his living-room sofa, alongside his small son Tatico in plaid bedroom slippers, each playing his guitar. A background TV beams cartoons.

Pascal is reflected in the gleaming hood of a big new Mercedes, which is parked among grapevines.

Julio is behind a pair of white plaster eagles guarding the grilled entrance of his glitzy new villa.

(These last two pictures tell you, This is how we spent Sony's money.)

And finally, a gang of little rascals, the musicians' sons, clambering on the wooden wheel of an old Gypsy caravan. The album is dedicated to these boys (the daughters are not included in the photograph): "To all the children who want to accompany us on the great musical voyage of the Gypsies . . ."

3

These songs are unearthly.

There's a musical rift that runs down the middle of France: Iberian Gypsies are bare-bones in their use of instrument: voice, palms of their hands, a guitar; Manush (of whom Django Reinhardt was the most renowned) and Tziganes from northern and eastern Europe have access to a richer repertoire of brass, strings, accordion.

Sony's money was able to broaden the Iberian Gypsy sound by importing trumpet, horn, trombone, clarinet, accordion, violin, cello. In addition, there are two guest singers: Parrita, a rumba superstar from Barcelona, and Khaled, a world-renowned king of Algerian *rai*.

But despite these well-chosen embellishments, the power of Tekameli remains in its naked voices. "I have a friend who records at the Barbican Center in London for Gergiev," says Garth. "He tells me he's rarely heard anything as good as my tape of these boys singing a capella in a church in Lucerne."

"These boys" sing solo and in chorus. They practice a polyphony more familiar to us from the Eastern Church, and their voices are eerily moving. They whisper, implore, soar, stutter, rasp. The singers range from Pascal Valles, whose Wagnerian heft would not sound out of place at the Metropolitan Opera, to Moïse Espinas, who has the torn bruised wail prized by flamenco.

Although the CD is marketed as "world music," in fact, from the opening song, "Mis Hermanos," in which the singers whisper their awe at hearing their fellow-congregants, their "brothers" in the *Assemblée,* weep with joy at God's greatness, these songs are uncompromisingly sectarian. The bulk of the album is hymns from the Pentacostalist Church which Tekameli and their French collaborators have adapted, although there is also an extract from a Catholic mass from Seville. The songs speak of religious ecstasy, terror, remorse, invoke Jesus's "*Eli, eli, lama sabachthani?*" and Saul's conversion on the road to Damascus, and they speak of their adoration of the Virgin Mary and of the mystical fellowship of Gypsies.

There are love songs among the hymns, but even Tekameli's love songs are frosted with a disconcerting chastity: "When I saw her pass, her hair was tangled, Mother of God, how beautiful she is!" or "You watch me with your face of a saint." The beloved is a "star" who lights the singer's dark path: she is remote, pure, unattainable.

One of the most affecting of the songs—a song powerfully jolted by Khaled's added track of Arabic *rai*—is called "O Madre," and it concludes with the singer's swearing in a heartbroken, voice-broken wail that gutters to a whisper that he will return to his mother a changed man, because he can neither live nor die without her. "O Madre" is a song you can imagine Elvis Presley or Roy Orbison singing—the self-lacerating lament of a dreamy mama's boy who is too wounded to grow up.

But there are other songs on *Ida y Vuelta* which make you realize that you are eavesdropping on a complex world based on ancient and, to most consumers of pop music, utterly alien values—a world whose sources of power and meaning might be symbolized in the white horse and the golden rooster.

"La Novia" is Tekameli's trump card. It is, essentially, an act of Promethean theft. "La Novia" is Tekameli's adaptation of a traditional Spanish Gypsy wedding song, and weddings are the most sacred of Gypsy rites. The song celebrates and sanctifies the bringing of a Gypsy girl to marriage according to *"la loi gitane."* One voice begins, others join, there's an intricate weave of voices, a polyphonic relay of key words and phrases. The sentence chanted over and over and over, shouted with fierce exultation, is *"Por ella es la honra de su familia* (For she is the honor of her family)."

It struck me, listening to "La Novia," that it had been a long time since I'd heard the word "honor" in any modern language, that it seemed an aristocratic vestige of a warrior society, which meant that in our own world, it survived mainly among men young, poor, and aimless enough to enjoy a fight. But "La Novia" speaks of female honor. And in what, I wondered, for Perpignan Gypsies —a society notoriously disparaging of women—does a woman's "honor" consist, save her proven chastity?

It was a couple of months before I discovered that the more specific answer lay in the song's dropped allusion to the bride's *"panuelito"* (the handkerchief). The *panuelito,* it turned out, referred to the central rite of a Spanish Gypsy wedding, in which the intended bride is taken off to a room and laid out on a table. An old woman—an accredited official, chosen by the groom's family—then examines the girl's hymen to make sure it is intact, while the girl's female in-laws watch. (I've heard different accounts, including from Gypsy brides, as to whether the old woman actually penetrates the girl with her fingers or not, but since it's hymenal blood that's required, she surely must.)

The handkerchief, dabbed in the virgin's blood, is then paraded before the wedding crowd, waved aloft to the triumphant shouts of *"la novia,"* and the bride is borne around the room on her brothers' shoulders. Only now, once the bride's virginity has been confirmed, can the wedding proceed. Only with this bloody voucher is the marriage deemed valid.

The "handkerchief" became briefly infamous in France, when the magazine *Télérama* published a photo-essay of a St. Jacques bride undergoing this most intimate ceremony. For months after the *Télérama* article, I was told by people like Guy Bertrand to tread carefully in St. Jacques, since Gypsies were still up in arms about their betrayal by the *paia* photojournalist who'd splashed one of their maidens, legs spread like a porn star, across the pages of a mass-market weekly.

Later, Tekameli's bassist Jeannot and his wife, Incarnacion, show me the video of their own wedding, including the *panuelito,* in which the seventeen-year-old bride, in long white pearl-studded dress, is laid out on the table, rigid with fear. Jeannot declares himself to be all in favor of this ceremony, which he mockingly refers to as "the Kleenex," and which is a tribute to the good reputation both of the bride's family and of the groom (a divorced man, for instance, is not entitled to a "handkerchief"). "I wouldn't have had her, without," he laughs.

Another afternoon, I listen to "La Novia" with Joseph Poubil at the Casa Musicale. Joseph, who has played bass and *cajon* in all the best Gypsy bands in Perpignan, including Tekameli, is something of a Gypsyologist. Since earliest childhood, he tells me, he collected words of Kalo, pieces of Gypsy lore, and when he pronounces the word "Gitan," it's in a voice husky with reverence, as of someone cradling an amulet in his palm.

Joseph is the likeliest embodiment of what Stéphane Henri calls "Gypsy modernity." Not only does he work a nine-to-five job at the Casa, where he's learned to run the state-of-the-art recording equipment—and therefore he has a marketable skill, he also is the only Gypsy I know who "lets" his pretty young wife wear jeans, and brings her along on his evening entertainments. To spot Joseph at the theater with Olivia, now pregnant with their second child, is a sight unknown among other Perpignan marrieds. He, laughing, leaning close, whispering in her ear, has the air of a young man still courting, and she, smiling, looks as if she likes what he's telling her.

I ask Joseph about the line in "La Novia" where the bride's said to bring "honor" to her family.

He smiles, but his light-brown eyes are brimming with tears.

"You know what happens to me when I hear that line?"

Joseph rolls up the sleeve of his nylon sports shirt, and shows me that his slim olive arm has come out in goose bumps.

I have listened to a lot of the music favored by other Perpignan kids, "French" kids, whose parents come from Bordeaux and Lille and Marseille and Réunion. They play for me songs by French hip-hop groups like Assassin and NTM, or by the Toulouse collective Zebda, who take an art form invented by young American "minorities," and use it to describe the daily hassles, humiliations, and recreational pleasures peculiar to young European "minorities."

But Tekameli belongs to another planet, another century.

No "French" kid listens to *Ida y Vuelta,* because for most "French" pop-music fans, bridal virginity is no longer an issue that brings happy tears to their eyes.

What *Ida y Vuelta* represents is a music that is both "world" in its hybridity—Afro-Caribbean beat, Spanish and Gitan lyrics, an Anglo-Saxon Protestant cult—and forbiddingly local. It is a conundrum as flagrant as the centerfold's deck of tarot-card talismans: Ferris wheel, rooster, white horse, a Mercedes-Benz among the beachy grapevines; as the lead votive prayers to the Celtic water nymphs composed in Iberian, transcribed into Latin and Greek, and now lost. A sound that is as "other" as Siberian throat-singing, and yet was born in the south of France.

4

For a year, when I went to the great cities of the Western world, I saw Tekameli's golden fairy wheel plastered all over Tower, Virgin, HMV stores in Times Square, Montparnasse, Piccadilly Circus. I heard on television ads the snatch of "O Madre" that Sony was using to sell its new Walkman.

But in Perpignan, silence.

An article in the local newspaper claimed that Tekameli was nowadays so busy touring Sweden, Belgium, Australia, that they rarely could be found in their ungrateful hometown. "Prophets in their own country," explained one music promoter.

The house listed on *Ida y Vuelta* as the group's headquarters was shuttered closed.

Even Garth, who had lots of old war stories about taking Tekameli on tour, seemed to have finally gotten fed up and lost touch with them.

I thought I had missed Tekameli, that they had moved away somewhere northern, rich, and cold, to be famous.

I imagined them with their own recording studio in Stockholm.

5

Le Sud is one of the hip restaurants in Perpignan.

It serves Mediterranean food in an old Spanish palace across the street from St. Jacques's Caserne, where you sit in a courtyard festooned in hanging pots of flowers and painted Moroccan lanterns.

After dinner, two musicians stroll from table to table. Jérôme, who has the jittery eyes of a horse about to bolt, wears floral polyester and a Bee Gees hairdo. Jérôme seems to take a perverse pleasure in serenading the surliest or most embarrassable diners, leaning close and smiling into eyes desperate to avoid his. His fellow-guitarist, a dapper old gentleman named Francisquet, dressed in a straw hat and a jaunty suit, exudes a discreet Latin elegance.

They play Gypsy rumba, Jérôme singing in a voice suitably ravaged. His guitar looks as if it's been pieced together after a car crash, but he has this demon-quick way of snapping his long slim fingers against the guitar's body in speedy syncopated riffs that is utterly his own.

We chat; Jérôme hands me his card. It's the Tekameli Ferris wheel.

"Do you know Tekameli?" I ask, immensely excited.

Jérôme is nonchalant. "Sure, I started them."

At this point, I don't know much about Gypsy ways. To me, music is still a business of record-label contracts, rehearsal studios in world capitals, producers putting together a marketable sound. Jérôme's claim I take as seriously as when the shriveled ancient in the boxing club tells you he taught Joe Louis. But when I go home to my collection of Perpignan Gypsy CDs, I learn from the liner notes that Jérôme Espinas—hailed as one of the best local practitioners of the flamenco *cante jondo*—was in fact the founder of Tekameli, which originally consisted of Jérôme and his three nephews, Salomon, Moïse, and Jérémie, who later dropped out because he was too bad a junkie, and that one of the most hair-raising tracks on *De San Jaume Son* is of Jérôme, his voice ten years younger, singing a fandango.

Over the next few years, I meet the most unexpected people, a secret society of "French," usually middle-aged playboys of immense worldliness, who turn out to be well acquainted with Jérôme. I am told that he is both an insatiable libertine ("an animal") and the most gifted of musicians, who might have gone far, if he hadn't been "completely insane."

6

During my early encounters with Gypsies, I often had moments of anti-epiphany, revelations of an almost unbridgable divergence in assumptions and expectations, a mutual incomprehension aggravated by the fact that we each spoke a different kind of bad French.

It was a contrast of modern bourgeois and ancient aristocratic. There were things I found essential—order, reliability, discipline—that meant nothing to them. Their ruling virtue of *bella figura*—being seen as open-handed, beautifully adorned, loyal—I didn't care about, at least not in the same way they did.

My first anti-epiphany occurred another night at Le Sud, when I asked Jérôme if he played there often. Of course, it's his job. There are three or four chic Perpignan restaurants that hire him to play. Every night he performs at one of them.

"I'd love to hear you again," I venture. "Which nights do you come to Le Sud?"

He looks blank. I try to rephrase the question.

Finally, he answers, with an airy wave of the hand, "When I think of it."

Jérôme's remembering to show up at his job—inspired by the need for instant cash, or a desire to get out of the house—is fairly haphazard. One wintry night, chased by the howling Tramontane, Jérôme and Francisquet and my husband and I all find ourselves huddled outside the shuttered door of Al Tres, Jérôme and Francisquet not having known or remembered that the restaurant was closed till Easter.

Jérôme never seems to recognize me from one encounter to the next, even when I begin to be brought back to his house by family members, but each time he is equally gallant. For a long time, this was my experience of Perpignan Gypsies. Although there were presumably not that many New York journalists wanting to write about Gypsy music in St. Jacques, every time I bumped into Titou or Nelly or Sephora, although friendly, they appeared to have only the dimmest recollection of ever having seen me before, and if I passed them in the street and didn't actually make a point of going up and reintroducing myself, they would stare right through me.

Even though I came from what they all professed to be the center of the world, the source of whatever they loved, whether the old Hollywood stars Francisquet favored (Jee-*mee* Stee-*art*; Ay-*wa* Gard-*nair*; Keem No-*wack*) or the Nike sneakers and Adidas tracksuits his grandchildren craved, the reality of a *paia*, I concluded, must be pale and spectral, compared to their own urgencies.

In fact, I was wrong: the Gypsies' cool indifference, their apparent inability to recognize me, was simply the self-defense of undesirables, an instinct to snub you before you had a chance to snub them. As I later discovered, they knew me even more keenly than I knew them, and could tell me exactly which day and in whose company I had passed down their street. Though they seemed to take small notice of me when I came, if I didn't come, they missed me, and worried that I was sick or that they had done something to offend me.

7

For months, I listened hypnotically to *Ida y Vuelta,* while pursuing Tekameli leads and Gypsy research on the side. I left phone messages on dead voice mails. I spoke to musicians' daughters, nephews, cousins-in-law, who told me to call back later, by which time the telephone had been cut off. In a perfect emblem of futility, I sent letters composed in painstaking schoolgirl French to men I later discovered were illiterate. I received a charming note from Alain Tarrius, the sociologist of Perpignan outcasts, inviting me to his house up the Tet valley on such-and-such a day, but having driven two hours, was told he had gone away, and never again received an answer.

I moped, I fretted, I sulked, I listened some more to *Ida y Vuelta,* and wondered if I played it backward would I hear that Jérémie was dead. Jeff at Lolita Disques told me I had to go to the *Assemblée,* so I did. He drew a map leading to the Life and Light Church, uphill from the Place Cassanyes, a hole-in-the-wall storefront that didn't advertise its function or hours, since anybody who needed to know, knew.

I went one Wednesday night, and found the long room packed with a hundred Gypsies. It reminded me of Orthodox synagogues on the Upper West Side of Manhattan, both because the men sat with the men and the women with the women, and because the majority of the congregants were in their early twenties, an anomaly suggesting that people came to church to find marriage partners. The men rose to testify to the power of God's healing love, an assortment of pastors shouted their sermons in fierce Gitan, and there was, gospel-style, an unbroken unity between the hymns sung here—

drowned out, unfortunately, by synthesizers—and the rumba you heard from St. Jacques apartments and cars, which suggested that the religion was still red hot and kicking.

I have been to evangelist meetings in Mexico and Sicily, but here in Perpignan there was perhaps even less text, an even starker absence of references to the Bible. You had the impression of an oral religion which had not yet been codified, a gospel, as in Jesus's preachings, whose intended audience was poor, illiterate, broken, sick.

And indeed, considering that most of the congregants were in the flower of youth, there was a heavy emphasis on illness. If premodern appeals to faith hinge on the deal— what God's going to do for you in return for your fealty—at Life and Light, the promised payback was not wealth or a good harvest or military hegemony, it was strictly medical. God's special attraction was as a healer of disease. As congregants rose to attest to miraculous cures, you had the impression of a people in really wretched health.

I sat in a chair by the door, and as the only non-Gypsy in the room, the only person wearing scarlet, yellow, and hot-blue in a sea of black, felt as usual in St. Jacques glaringly invisible. There wasn't even a surreptitious glance my way. Two-thirds through the service, a young man came in, grabbed the free chair next to mine, and only then, seeing me, started back in an involuntary fright, the appalled recoil of a toddler who's just realized that the adult whose knees he's reaching for isn't his mother.

It was then that I understood something of the reality behind Gypsy defiance, Gypsy insults, Gypsy jeers. St. Jacques Gypsies are in fact far more scared of non-Gypsies than even the timidest non-Gypsy is of them. I was reminded of visiting the St. Jacques nursery school with Stéphane Henri, when catching sight of us the three-year-old ran shrieking to hide in her teacher's skirt.

"There's always one who starts crying when she sees a *paio*," Stéphane Henri had said philosophically. "Later they try to keep a little more cool about it."

∽

In the end, it's a door-to-door salesman who introduces me to Tekameli.

Chapter Five

1

We live in the commune of Sainte Marie.

Sainte Marie is a walled medieval village on the salt plain of the Salanque, fifteen kilometers east of Perpignan, and built in the rough porridge of river-bed stones and herring-bone zigzags of red brick that is known as *cayrou*. Most of the people who live in Sainte Marie are retired farmworkers or artisans. There are old ladies in housecoats, with lovely false teeth, old men in plaid bedroom slippers who like to potter in their kitchen gardens or sit on a sunny bench and watch the noonday bus to Perpignan go by.

There are a couple of families of Manush Gypsies who have houses in the village—in my daughter's kindergarten, briefly, there was Johnny Steynbach, who was three years older than the other children, because his family was so often on the road, and who went to school in the winter (when his mother thought of it) and who left every spring.

Sainte Marie, like all the villages along this coast, has spawned a modern twin—Sainte Marie Plage, a complex of beachside condos and fast-food shacks and novelty stores that are boarded up eight months a year. The people who live in Sainte Marie Plage year-round tend to be young and fast. There are stories of drug deals and police raids.

Perpignan is not yet a magnetic-enough job center to have turned such outlying villages into a commuter belt. At lunchtime and in the evening in Sainte Marie, men in blue overalls ride their bicycles home from work in the fields, and until the summer tourists arrive, the only traffic jams are from tractors. On weekends, I see my son's nursery-school teacher, alongside the other women, wringing out her laundry in the stone basin of the village washhouse.

Teenagers in Sainte Marie get sidelined early into vocational school. Hairdresser for girls, plumbing or electrician for boys. They leave school at sixteen, and then have little to do but hang out at the bus stop, waiting for summer, when Parisian kids come down and steal the girls. There is a low buzz of delinquency, which mostly serves to keep the extreme-right-wing National Front vote high, and which is the more annoying since the "perpetrators" know their victims are as hard-up as they are. Delinquency is little more than a recycling of the same battered goods. The kids down the block steal Florian's motorbike, which means Florian can no longer get to work; Florian and his cousin hot-wire someone else's car. Florian, whose father has abandoned the family and whose mother is in and out of the local psychiatric hospital, offers one insight into low-level European anti-Semitism. When asked by his grandmother why he'd painted a swastika on a wall, he said he didn't know what it meant, but he knew it was the worst thing he could think of, and he figured if he did it often enough, he'd get sent to reform school, where at least he'd get regular meals.

Hajiba Mohib, who lives in a suburban villa by the canal,

belongs to Sainte Marie's small professional class. Hajiba is one of my closest friends in Roussillon—a tall, stately woman in her late thirties with enormous round eyes like black grapes and an air of barely suppressed drama altogether out of proportion to village life. She was eight years old, the second of seven sisters and a brother, when her family emigrated from Morocco to a housing project outside Strasbourg.

Hajiba and her siblings inhabit a world you don't much hear about in France, but which you might describe as yuppie *Maghrebin*. *Maghrebin* is the French term for Arabs originating from the Maghreb, or North Africa. It's a world in which young people have jobs in the new economy of computers, advertising, tourism, telecommunications, in which they sometimes marry fellow-Muslims, sometimes don't, and are equally likely to name their children "Adnan" or "Bryan." They speak Arabic to their elders, but can't read it, they drink wine and eat sausage, but feel guilty when they do, and they have fond memories of childhood Ramadans, though they don't keep the fast themselves. It's a cultural positioning similar to American Jews of a previous generation, before faith came back in style, but in fact, it's harder than it looks.

These are people whose suave conviviality covers the trauma of having grown up in the squeeze of two contradictory pressures: while the larger society of teachers, neighbors, school friends, and employers demanded that you expunge your origins and become invisibly French, at home, and on summer trips back to your family's native village, you were expected to erase the guilt of your parents' immigration by proving yourself a perfect Arab Muslim.

It's a strain, being constantly watched with a critical eye by French people, ready to think all Arabs are hoodlums, welfare bums, or, more recently, fundamentalist suicide-bombers, or by other Arabs, ready to deem you a whore because your skirt's too short and somebody saw you getting out of a boy's car one night. Scratch a little deeper into merry family reunions, and you'll find a father who hasn't spoken to his daughter in twenty years because she lives with a Frenchman, a nephew who's joined the Muslim Brotherhood.

Hajiba's common-law husband (her first husband was a Moroccan who wouldn't give her a divorce) is Frédéric Guillem, a Catalan from a Spanish anarchist family. Like many of the people I meet in Roussillon, Hajiba and Frédéric live in the cracks between the old Mediterranean world, which values family, tradition, respect, and peace of mind, and the new world of SUVs, gated communities, and throw-away jobs. Frédéric, who likes to play the guitar but is good at number-crunching, works a job he finds immoral, lending money to already over-endebted civil servants.

Work, in a fallen world, is what you do to eat, but your real life is at home. I have seen Frédéric cut short a business meeting in order to run his mother to the supermarket. Hajiba works office jobs the way other people in Roussillon pick grapes for a season: if the family is short of cash for Christmas, she will sell CD-ROMs or cell-phone subscriptions. But, on the whole, she'd rather stay home. She didn't like having to raise her six younger siblings while her parents worked their corner grocery store into a successful catering business, and she wants her own daughters to return from school to a house warm with kitchen smells, a mother ready to hear their news.

At weekends, Frédéric cooks a stew from the wild boar his grandfather hunted. Hajiba prepares a Moroccan feast that takes two days to cook and three days to eat. Their dinner parties last till breakfast.

When I first meet the Guillem-Mohibs, Frédéric has not yet been promoted to regional chief of the loan company. He is still moonlighting to make ends meet, sometimes as a security guard, sometimes as a door-to-door salesman. One of his jobs was selling cable-TV subscriptions to Gypsies. Frédéric is shy but kind and it's he who offers to take me around St. Jacques, chasing down some of the musicians he'd encountered on his rounds.

Winter ends early in Roussillon. Spring is raw, wet, gray, but each year there comes a moment, shockingly early—late January, early February—when the first mimosas are in chemical-yellow bloom, and you know you've turned the corner.

Today is such a corner. It's early February, the first hot day of the new year. St. Jacques has its own indefinable Mediterranean slum-smell, and the noonday heat is uncorking it from gutters, empty lots, entryways. If I were landed blindfolded and earplugged in St. Jacques, I would know it by this dry, crumbly, acrid scent of building rubble, rooster, cat piss, rotting garbage. One day—maybe after the high-speed railway from Barcelona to Paris reaches Perpignan—the smell will be gone, and the Gypsies, too, and St. Jacques will be one more renovated quarter in a southern French town with boutiques selling lavender oil and espadrilles. And on All Saints' Day, who then will come back to wail over the Gypsy dead, in the graveyards of St. Martin, St. Antoine, St. Jacques?

Pockmarked walls and front doors are covered in chalked lists of which-girl-loves-which-boy: Kelly=A; Tatiana=J;

Vanessa=F; Sabrina=B. Unlike most twelve-year-olds, these poor girls are probably going to have to marry their crushes.

The black-clad women sit in chairs on the street, the children play in the rubble of a torn-down house; the women lean from upstairs windows, gossip between laundry lines, the men stand in a huddle at a corner, or talk leaning out of parked cars. Roosters crowing, arguments, flamenco, salsa, rumba blaring from open windows, Moïse Espinas swearing in a hoarse wail that he will come back to his mother a changed man.

St. Jacques was one of Frédéric's beats last year.

"Were people friendly?"

"Sure, I was offering something they wanted. The women are home all day, they watch TV day and night, and the reception in those rabbit-hutch apartments is terrible. When they found out where I was from, the whole family would descend, it was, *Amigo, amigo*. The women would feed me, the men would pass me the guitar, or try to sell me something in return: a pair of shoes, a radio. These Gypsies are still moving, even if they live in houses. The men go off to Hungary, Poland, they buy used cars, they replace the engines, they resell them in France. Often, I would return and find out that the whole family had decamped to Lille or Nancy, and nobody knew when they'd be back."

Each Gypsy neighborhood was different, he explained. In St. Jacques, the streets were filthy, they threw their garbage out the window, but inside, the apartments were immaculate, "as in Spain." In Haut Vernet, there were the "Baptists," whose men never cut their hair or beards, where people were wild but gentle. There, the houses were dirty, the people primitive, but intensely evangelized. Their first concern was if there were "adult" programs on cable, because they didn't want their children seeing filth. Behind was another Gypsy housing project, the infamous Cité Bellus, where men settled differences with switchblades, but even there he'd never had trouble.

"And did you ever have trouble getting them to pay up?" I ask hesitantly, not liking to repeat racist slurs. Frédéric grins. "No problem. It was simple: They *never* paid. What I learned later was that this was often the second, third, fourth time these families had had cable installed. Each plan's different: sometimes it's six months free, and another couple of months before they actually get round to cutting it off. Can you imagine being a cable servicemen sent to St. Jacques? You get out there to disconnect the service, all the men surround you, what do you think you're doing, suddenly there are knives . . .

"They are very sly, they've got all kinds of tricks to fool *paios*. I'd be sitting at the table, filling out the forms, what's your name, and the woman would say, Giminez, and her husband would say, No, no, not Giminez, you used that last time. Each woman has three last names: her mother's maiden name, her father's name, and her husband's name, which means three times as many welfare benefits, and three times as good a chance of escaping debts."

Frédéric relays these anecdotes with the amused wonder of someone unconquerably law-abiding, an inheritance from his Spanish anarchist grandfather, he jokes. He would be a Gypsy if he could, but his inveterate correctness instead has doomed him to a life of filing cabinets, mortgages, and pension plans.

We are looking first for Pitou Cargol. Pitou Cargol is as close as St. Jacques has to a godfather. He belongs to one of the first families in Roussillon to "receive the word of God," and he himself is a leading Pentacostalist pastor. Pitou Cargol is the man who chose Tekameli's name. He is the person to whom Guy Bertrand, the former professor of traditional music at the conservatory, went when he wanted to meet Gypsy musicians in Perpignan. He is also the mayor's official "mediator," the distributor of municipal goodies.

We knock on Pitou Cargol's door, which bears a brass plaque labeled MEDIATOR. There are already a few boys in black suits waiting to see the mediator.

His wife shouts down at us from an upstairs window. "Pitou's out."

"Where's he gone?"

"He went to get the red Skoda fixed."

Other women hanging out in the street join an enthusiastic debate about how long it might take to fix the red Skoda. They split hairs over which particular shifting hour of the day is the optimal time to find Pitou Cargol at home.

Next we go in search of Joseph "Mambo" Saadna, who is one of the four brothers of Els Rumberos Catalans. Els Rumberos Catalans is the most eminent and long-lived of Perpignan Gypsy bands and the only one which has successfully "crossed over." It's easy to find Spanish flamenco artists who have collaborated with jazz, rock, and even Arab-Andalou musicians, but French Catalan Gypsies are more hidebound. The Rumberos, however, have gone World, while sticking to their roots: Mambo and his brother Roberto for years have performed with Thierry Robin, a Northern French oud player whose band includes Arab-Persian instruments and a Rajasthani singer. Els Rumberos Catalans, with Thierry Robin, have toured worldwide, and commanded the biggest and most prestigious venues in Europe.

Mambo lives in the rue de Tracy, formerly "the Street of

False Witnesses," which is one of the slummiest alleys of St. Jacques. There is a gang of girls outside Mambo's door, who want to know, friendly, curious, what we're up to, and when we say we're looking for Mambo, a tall teenager with pale-green mulatto eyes boasts happily, "I'm his niece!" Again, a wife leans out of an upstairs window, and explains that Mambo's touring Holland, and won't be back for two weeks.

Other times, looking for Mambo, I tumble up these breakneck rotten tenement stairs, but Mambo's never home, Mambo's always on tour. And I realize that both for their left-behind families and for the musicians themselves, Mambo's playing a concert in Holland isn't much different from Tony or Chatou's bringing back a cannibalized Mercedes or a truckload of cheap track shoes from Poland.

Mambo, whom I never manage to see except in concert, is a devastatingly handsome man, mustachioed, debonair. Even though he is now a grandfather many times over, he is so handsome that it gets in the way of everything, just as if he were born a billionaire or blind.

From time to time people who don't like Mambo will tell me he's greedy and only goes where there's money, and I always think of Mambo's apartment, on the Street of False Witnesses. Inside, a slew of kids and a pale, haggard wife who looks decades older than he and sounds cross, but is simply worn out from having married too young and having had too many children too fast, one of whom, with a massive lolling head and an infant-sized body, is permanently strapped into a wheelchair so he won't hurt himself during his seizures—a child for whom it is a losing battle just to draw oxygen into his lungs.

The apartment is tiny but immaculate, geraniums in olive-oil cans at the window, and on the wall a Xerox blowup of Mambo with the other Rumberos. And you think, what does money *mean* in such a case? Is it any wonder, having played the same music since he was a child and living like shit, that he might like to see some before he dies?

2

Now we're looking for jittery-eyed Jérôme Espinas, who plays the chic restaurants of Perpignan, and his nephew Moïse, original founding member and lead singer of Teka-meli, and possessor of the greatest voice north of Barcelona. We head down to the rue des Carmes, to a row of houses built into the ramparts of the medieval Carmelite convent, opposite the baths, which are not as you might suppose a lovely hammam, but public showers for backpackers and tramps.

A woman is sitting on a chair outside her door, which Frédéric informs me is the house next-door-but-one to that of Moïse's mother-in-law. The woman has long sleek black hair tinged with gray, a rosy nut-brown face, sparkly brown eyes.

We knock at her neighbor's door. The woman watches, intrigued.

"Is Moïse's mother-in-law in?"

She goes blank. If Moïse's mother-in-law lives there, she is unaware of the fact.

Frédéric comes closer. "We're looking for Moïse Espinas."

In my day tagging along with Frédéric, I've noticed something peculiar to cultures which still keep the sexes apart. Frédéric talks, but it's me the women answer, angling past the man, and for the first time I see a flicker of curiosity, of something that might turn into sympathy, amusement, warmth.

Moïse Espinas? The grandmother is blandly ignorant, polite as if we've told her we're chasing butterflies. She has clearly never heard the name before in her life.

Frédéric tries one last time. "Does Moïse still live in that same apartment on Aristide Briand? Because I know he was thinking of moving . . ."

Now she brightens. "Oh no, he's still there," she informs me.

Later I discover that the woman of whom she betrayed so little knowledge is her sister, that Moïse is her nephew-in-law, and her husband is Francisquet, the elegant old guitarist in the straw hat who plays with Jérôme. The Gypsy method resembles the old Soviet system of no telephone directories: if you don't already know the person's number, you've got no business calling him.

3

Frédéric sniffs his way along Boulevard Aristide Briand, until he comes to a Moroccan restaurant called La Fantaisie, with a neon sign depicting an Arabian Nights–style oasis.

"I think it's this building." He checks the buzzers, and rings one. We climb two flights. A sleepy young woman in a dressing gown tells us through the chain-latched door that Moïse will be back at six.

At six, there's no Moïse, but we are invited in.

The apartment is spotless. There is a matching set of table, chairs, and sideboard in pearlescent blue laminate, a set of butter-yellow leather sofa and armchairs, and an armoire filled with glass collectibles, sets of wedding china, sports trophies. The television is blaring game shows; the stereo is blaring salsa. The living room is full of women and children.

There's a teenage girl, who is wearing silk pajamas and red leather boxing gloves. There are two young boys who are practicing martial-arts kicks. There is a baby in a playpen. And three ladies.

One, a severe, hood-eyed, straight-backed granny, has already been informed by her sister—the apple-cheeked lady—that two *paios* have come looking for her.

She is visiting her two daughters, who both live in this same building, and who are to become, did I but know, my best friends in Perpignan.

Linda, the mother of the girl-boxer and of the younger of the two boys, is thirty years old, tall and beautiful, with a dimpled white smile, hair done in a headdress of African braids, good makeup, and charm like a Mickey Finn. Her younger sister, Diane, small, bedraggled, has a sheepish grin. Two or three crucial teeth are missing, and those that remain are yellow or rotting brown.

The three women are thrown into a tizzy, half-excited, half-alarmed, by these foreign Tekameli fans showing up in their living room. (The public side of Gypsy musicians' lives, I am learning, rarely impinges upon the drab bubble of their home lives.) Moïse is still rehearsing, he's about to leave for a concert in Germany—they argue amongst themselves, mother and sisters, about whether to invite us to sit down, offer us a drink—rum? Coca-Cola? grenadine?—or whether it's more polite just to take my phone number and not detain me, since Moïse isn't here.

When she hears I come from New York, Diane, the smaller one, falls back on the sofa in a mock faint. "Take me with you!"

Her sister Linda is not so easily impressed. *They* come from Paris, she counters. I've been to Paris, of course? Not bad, is it? When they arrived in Perpignan as teenagers, they were in shock.

"I kept asking, 'But where's the subway?' 'There is no subway.' 'Let's go downtown.' 'This *is* downtown.' "

I mistake Linda for Moïse's wife, in the idea that the beauty queen belongs with the pop star, but Linda informs me with a proud laugh that she is a single mother. This is Linda's style: a quick, sharp-tongued frontal defiance, its aggressive edge tempered by the dazzling smile and loud laugh.

"I'm looking for a man, but the men here are useless," she says, shooting a provocative glance at Frédéric, who sinks deeper into his chair.

"Maybe you'd prefer a Parisian," I suggest.

The two sisters burst into scandalized, thigh-slapping laughter. I discover later that Linda's lifelong lover is indeed a Parisian.

The intercom buzzes, Linda answers. "Monsieur Espinas is wanted for an interview with a journalist from New York! Ha-ha-ha!" But now there is a flurried alarm in the air akin to that occasioned by our arrival. The man of the house is home, he's going to be angry about something.

I think of the Turkish novelist Latife Tekin's telling me of her shantytown childhood, "When the man returns at night, you pretend to be pleased, but meanwhile you are always thinking, He should leave so we can enjoy ourselves. When my father left the house, my mother would kiss the door. I say this not out of my good conscience, but because it's the truth."

4

And Moïse is in the room. He charges in, like a bull enter-
ing the arena, pawing the dust, swinging around at us with
a territorial glare. Grandmother Antoinette stands up to
leave, Linda too. Suddenly everyone is scurrying to make
room, to get out.

Frédéric and I apologize for intruding unannounced.

"No, no," Moïse growls, "I just want to see my baby."

He surges past us to the crib, plumps up pillows and
blanket, rearranges the toys, with a solicitude which silently
accuses the women in the house of negligence, then sweeps
his nine-month-old son into the air, father and child crowing
in joint satisfaction.

With his baby in his arms, he's ready to talk. I explain my
business: I'm an American journalist, and want to write
about Tekameli. Moïse relaxes into his habitual frown, and,
following St. Jacques etiquette, addresses Frédéric.

Moïse Espinas has a powerful stage persona of Mephistophelian menace, an aura of someone who is perpetually and
massively pissed-off. In his own living room, it's no less formidable: his features, his carriage, his manner of dressing all
merge into one concentrated scowl. He's dark bronze and
sinister handsome, with blue-black brush cut and goatee,
glowering V-shaped eyebrows. He is dressed, Gypsy-fashion,
in black T-shirt, black jacket, black trousers, black leather
coat, and black boots. The overall blackness is alleviated only
by bulky garnishings of gold—gold rings, gold medallions,
gold crucifix, and gold watch. You are reminded that Heath-
cliff in *Wuthering Heights* was said to be a Gypsy foundling.

The storm cloud over Moïse's head is an attribute that

appears neither to mount into actual violence nor to diminish into petulance. It's a while before I realize that Moïse's glare is merely tactical, the expression of an outraged innocence, in which you, the spectator, are occasionally invited, with a sidelong wink and grin, to collude.

My initial impression that Moïse is angry is aggravated, moreover, by the tonalities of Gitan: a language which, to an outsider, sounds as if it has no vowels, but is spat, snarled, squawked, sputtered in bullet-like gulps that seem to constitute a running dialogue between Accusation and Outraged Disavowal. For the first few months of our acquaintance, whenever Moïse and Diane, or Diane and Linda, or Diane and her mother, talk between themselves, I think they are quarreling. They are, but the combativeness is weightless, merely stylistic: Antoinette's calling her daughter a whore or Diane's calling her husband a stingy bastard has no more import than the waitress's calling you honey.

Moïse, when I first meet him, is twenty-eight years old—in Gypsy terms, a mature paterfamilias. When he's angry, his build appears burly, muscled, but when he's genial, his upper body goes cuddly as a stuffed bear. In all moods, there's a square solidity to him. You understand why women or children might like to snuggle up against his unreliable chest.

Moïse is quiet, but I soon find that one of the less explicable pleasures in the world is riding around in his smashed-up iridescent-aquamarine Kyoto sports car, Moïse with the driver's seat tipped back at a forty-five-degree recline, cruising at fifteen miles an hour through the back alleys of St. Jacques, Gypsy rumba blasting, Moïse singing along in a husky whisper, occasionally chatting through the open window with passersby, and hearing from other open windows of houses, cars, the exultant shout of "La Novia."

Moïse's in-laws think he's a sweetheart, unusually open-minded, gentle, and kind for a Gypsy man. His wife dotes on him, even when she's about to kick him out. Anybody who's worked with him professionally, on the other hand—from lighting technicians to sound engineers to his manager—is less charitable, but that might just be because Gypsy men think it's their business to jerk around non-Gypsy men.

Now that he knows we're customers, Moïse turns on the charm, flashing a guileless smile of deliciously even baby teeth. His body unwinds in rolling gestures, he's got this bounce-and-roll, this gleam in his eye, a hook of the Mephistophelian eyebrow, a showman's hustle.

The trouble is, for the longest while I can only understand about a third of what Moïse says. His wife Diane and her family can produce a respectable southern street French, although Linda is always accusing Diane of letting her French get Gitanized. Moïse's relation to French, however, is altogether different. To him, it's a distant second language, the appurtenance of *paios,* through whose bare stony porticoes the warmth of his Gitan keeps flooding.

You're a journalist, he asks me through the medium of Frédéric. Great, we're huge in the U.S., have you heard our Walkman ad, I'm off for a gig in Germany, they love us, they're asking where to send the flowers, let's not hang around talking, talk is boring, come by tomorrow, I'll take you to a rehearsal, you can meet the band.

This is the first and last time I get a sales pitch from Moïse, and yet even now I catch funny discordances, inadvertent signals that he is neither as worldly wise nor as ambitious as he would like you to believe.

Chapter Six

1

The Maison du Vernet is a community center. It is a concrete building painted in one of those schoolchildren's murals of happy faces and sunflowers that tend to embellish neighborhoods where drive-by shootings are a common occurrence and life expectancy for young males is a whole lot lower than the national average. Inside, there are notices tacked up on cork bulletin-boards, a receptionist behind sliding glass windows, teenagers and "seniors" hanging about in the lobby, who immediately latch on to a stranger for welcome distraction from the institutional scent of boredom and disinfectant. You could be in a mental-health ward or a halfway house for substance abusers. You are in Haut Vernet.

Haut Vernet is the end of a kilometer-long series of housing projects that line the road to the airport, an area that is Perpignan's version of what's called in French "the *banlieues*." The *banlieues* are the outskirts of a city, in postwar terms, what lies beyond the beltway, but in fact what they are is France's version of "inner city," a no-go zone of high-rise projects where the poor are stockaded. It's the *banlieues*—or, rather, urban planners' now regretted policy of relegating an immigrant workforce to purpose-built complexes, far from any more organic or mixed neighborhoods—that is blamed for many European social ills whether extreme-right racism or radical Islam.

The *banlieues* and their housing projects are places the French government periodically imposes curfews, where—in the more extreme cases—cars are set on fire and policemen are stoned. They are, by definition, inhabited by outsiders, not only the previous generation's cheap labor force, whether North African or Turk, but that generation's recalcitrant children, plus a thin residue of elderly French people who can't, or don't want to, get away, including the occasional communist who still stands by the Republican boilerplate about equality and fraternity.

In Perpignan, which has no industry and hence no labor, Haut Vernet is majority Gypsy. There is a mix of Andalusian, Manush, and Catalan, of whom some are Catholic, some are Pentacostalist, and some are Frédéric's longhaired Baptists. But there are also enough Turks and Arabs in Vernet for the city to be raising its first "official" mosque here (the others being mere hole-in-the-wall prayer houses), which is to be run by the most establishment of Perpignan's imams, and whose foundation-laying ceremony, attended by the city's chief rabbi and its Greek Orthodox and Roman Catholic bishops, was Mayor Alduy's canny response to September 11th.

If Perpignan were a northern French city, Haut Vernet would be a suicidally grim poverty trap, its cement weepy-gray in the rain and smog and mud. But Mediterranean light and landscape give shoddy developers a break: sunshine, orange trees, date palms, merry pennants of laundry, and views to the south of the high green Pyrenees, while to the west—just beyond the airport—opens a Monument Valley of rugged limestone buttes and canyons. For anybody belonging to St. Jacques, this is enemy territory, for the Gypsies of Haut Vernet are Bloods to St. Jacques's Crips. It's part of Tekameli's legend that they made peace between the two gangs.

I park next to Moïse's battered Kyoto, alongside the BMW and Mercedes cars of the other band members, who are waiting in the lot. Here is the gang: Pascal Valles, Tato Garcia, Jeannot Soler, Julio Bermudez, Moïse's brother Salomon, and a young *cajon*-player called Thierry Poubil, picked up from Rumba Mayor. Moïse has brought along his nine-year-old son, Kevin.

2

Laurent, the assistant director of Haut Vernet's community center, shows the boys into the rehearsal studio, which lies just past an arts-and-crafts room where elderly residents are crocheting afghans.

"Clean," remarks Jeannot, appreciatively.

"Yeah, the last band didn't trash it like you slobs," Laurent retorts.

NO SMOKING signs are prominent; the men instantly light up. Jeannot rolls a hash-and-tobacco joint and goes increasingly yellow. Moïse hazes Thierry, whom he introduces as *"Aspirador,"* "because his nose is a vacuum cleaner."

They are recording a demo to promote their German gig. They add voices, in turns. Tato, Tekameli's extremely gifted flamenco-style guitarist, plays a new track. Tato, a man with a torso overmuscled like a minotaur, is morose. The reason, I later discover, is that Moïse and Jeannot have just fired from the band a French violinist called Caro whom Guy Bertrand had brought in, and with whom Tato is having an affair.

"I didn't want Tato's wife getting mad at us," explains Moïse some months later, after Tato himself has quit the group and formed his own fusion band with Caro and a couple of younger St. Jacques rumba players. Garth's explanation is a little different: "They couldn't handle a chick."

Today the band is recording an old song they've revamped, but nobody can remember the words.

Salomon, the singer, hems and haws in search of the vanished lyrics, one arm wrapped around Thierry, while his palm beats the rhythm on Thierry's thigh.

Part of the problem is that the song is in Spanish, a language none of them knows all that well.

"Why do you sing in Spanish?" I ask Salomon.

He looks at me as if I'm very stupid. "Because the song's in Spanish."

"But wasn't it you who wrote the song?"

To this, there's no answer. The song is written in Spanish because Spanish is the language of rumba, just as German-speaking Mozart's opera about a Spanish libertine is written in Italian, since Italian is the language of opera.

Moïse takes a seat beside me, snuggling his son Kevin in his lap. Kevin (Ke-*veen,* it's pronounced in French, and is a name so popular among children his age that school classes have a Kevin D., Kevin G., Kevin M.) is a caramel-colored child with curly eyelashes that he knows how to use. He's a smart, friendly boy, who likes to lecture you on his favorite subjects: full contact, an art similar to Thai kickboxing, of which he's a national champion; soccer (he has his own neighborhood team); card tricks, of which he is eager to teach you the secrets; and cockfighting. He has the air of a benevolent diplomat. If he weren't a Gypsy, he'd be the class valedictorian.

But when Moïse stops nibbling on his son's ear and turns to polite conversation with the visitor from New York, Kevin, annoyed, tumbles from his father's lap and spins without warning into a full-contact kick.

Moïse, caught on the chin, glares. "Beat it, brat. Why aren't you in school today?"

"Mama didn't wake up in time." They came back late from a full-contact match in Montpellier, Kevin explains.

Moïse turns back to me. "This kid's a pest. You come from New York? New York's my dream. I can just see myself there. I have a *horror* of the mountains, of the country. For me, it's downtown, big cities all the way."

"So you're doing a concert in Germany next week. Which city?"

Moïse hasn't a clue. He appeals to the rest of the band in vain. None of them knows where in Germany they're playing nor, once they're back, will they know where they've been. Jeannot, the most clued-in, grins, "To us, it's just a long train ride," on which they play cards to make the time pass.

My question has opened up the gulf between *paia* and Gypsy, although in this case the gulf is between their experience and my inexperience. This, after all, is a musician's life, a succession of gigs whose locations are immaterial, and of which they retain only occasional recollections of scrapes they got into, the time the car broke down, or the hotel caught on fire, or the girl's boyfriend showed up.

All the rest is their manager Guy Bertrand's job. It's Guy who holds passports and bank accounts, who arranges their songs and decides where to sell them. If Moïse finds himself broke on a Saturday night, it's Guy he calls up for an "advance." It's even Guy who organizes Kevin's trips to his full-contact matches, or who, when Diane goes to Paris, picks her up from the Gare de Lyon, and deposits her safely at her aunt's apartment.

Kevin leans over, confidentially. "You know Guy?"

"I've met him."

"Isn't he an ugly bastard, with his faggot ponytail?"

"Shush," says his father.

"Can't have it all," smirks Jeannot, who's cute and knows it.

3

Tekameli's story, as told by Moïse and Jeannot, unfolds over coffee breaks during rehearsals, and in an empty working-man's bar by the fairground on the banks of the Tet.

Moïse Espinas, who was born in 1971, comes from a well-known St. Jacques family. His father is called "Trente" Cargol (Thirty Snail). Because the welfare system favors single mothers, St. Jacques Gypsies no longer have legal marriages, and children take their mother's name. Dr. Morcrette, my pediatrician friend, reports that her patients—women who "are monogamous for life"—unanimously insist their babies have no father, although they are equally quick to affirm that the non-father is free of AIDS or hepatitis.

"This is how my father got to be called 'Trente,' " Moïse relates. "One day, as a boy, he was fighting with his mother, when he saw his father coming. He jumped on his Solex 45 to get away, but the motorbike had no power. An old Gypsy was standing watching him, he says, 'Where you think you're going, little Gypsy, at *trente a l'hora* [30 kilometers an hour]?' The name stuck." In the '60s, Trente Cargol caught the evangelical bug. He became a pastor and a composer of hymns in the Pentacostalist church. He wrote songs that "lifted" sickness and he was responsible for curing many drug addicts. He also played rumba.

Moïse's mother, too, came from a musical dynasty, in which the men played, and the women danced. Moïse's wife Diane says her mother-in-law is a stunning dancer but, unlike in Spanish flamenco families, St. Jacques Gypsy women are not allowed to perform. When I ask Moïse, he says, dismissively, "She's an old lady." How old? Forty-three.

His mother's brother is the dandy Jérôme, who plays rumba in restaurants, when he thinks of it.

"When I was little, my uncle Jérôme kept asking me did I want to sing. *'Canta! Canta!'* But I didn't dare." (This is a traditional formula, I learn, expressing both an appropriate deference toward the talent of the elder and a fear of music's power, like Moses' taking off his shoes before the burning bush. Jérôme, too, tells me in similar words of his own musician father's having urged him to play the guitar: " 'Take it, take it.' I said, 'No, I don't want to.' I took it.") "Finally I began singing, all by myself, in the hall of our building, where it made a good echo. Then I sang canticles in church. When I was still a kid, thirteen, fourteen, my uncle Jérôme and I started playing together in cafés and bars, and we were joined by my brothers Salomon and Jérémie. In 1989, I was in the Place Cassanyes, and I saw a Gitan called Pitou Cargol, who introduced me to this professor from Toulouse who knew music."

Guy Bertrand picked the best of Perpignan's musicians, including some older stars who'd played with Manitas del Plata, forming them into new groups, and showing them how to develop and refine their own indigenous brand of music. Throughout the early to mid-'90s, he recorded four CDs of Perpignan Gypsy bands for the record label Al Sur.

Moïse's first exposure to a wider audience was when Guy Bertrand took a busload of his protégés to play a festival at Nantes. It was the moment of revelation.

"I had never performed in 'public,' before French people. When it came time to go out on stage, my knees trembled so hard I fell flat on my face, the audience laughed, and I did too. I sang, and it pleased me, and I thought, I could get a taste for this, this beats singing in the hallway. It was then I decided that I wanted to go far. For a few more years it was brothers and uncles. Then I met this skinny little Gypsy"—he nudges Jeannot—"who interested me a lot."

Jeannot, who belongs to the rival turf of Haut Vernet, comes from a different world from the St. Jacobins. His own family is at once more mainstream—one cousin is a computer programmer, another a sales representative—and more deeply imbued in Roussillon Gypsies' older rural traditions, of which he is proud. Jeannot's grandfather and his uncles are horse-breeders who buy and sell their horses at fairs all over Europe. An aunt and her husband and daughter are gamekeepers who run a shoot up in the mountains.

Jeannot's clan is still seminomadic. "Each family owns three or four properties. They'll buy a house in Bordeaux, plots of land in Alicante, Murcia, Almeria. They spend three months here, three months there, a month somewhere else. They move in anywhere from ten to thirty caravans, with their hunting dogs and their horses. One of my uncles has a brand-new villa behind Vernet, but the family doesn't live in it. They come in to use the kitchen, the shower, the WC, but they sleep in the caravan, and live in the open air."

Jeannot grew up in the projects of Haut Vernet. His pastor-father is a prison chaplain. Like Moïse's father, he is a charismatic "saver of souls": "He converted a whole family of drug-dealers, father, uncles, sons, nephews, now they're all healthy and church-going!"

Jeannot's father also has an extremely desirable job distributing public housing, a job which has enabled Jeannot to lay claim to the top floor of an Haut Vernet apartment building—three normal-sized apartments knocked together, with wraparound balconies offering 360-degree views of mountains and coast.

"I like to dominate the terrain," Jeannot jokes, the day he shows me around his new spread. "You want an apartment, Fernande? I'll take you to my dad, he'll get you a nice big place, subsidized rent. No problem."

The marriage between Jeannot of Haut Vernet and Moïse of St. Jacques was hard to consummate. "There were jealousies to be overcome," admits Jeannot. "I'd always considered myself the singer. It was hard to say, Fine, I'll play bass. And then, because Haut Vernet and St. Jacques were enemy camps, we were starting from zero. Tekameli has really moved things along between these two rival communities. We have shown upcoming kids how to resolve their conflicts. And we have changed the low opinion that people in Perpignan have of us Gypsies."

But their biggest challenge, Moïse adds, came from Gypsy elders. "At first, we were playing little love songs, like everybody else, but then we got the urge to play our religious music, and that was a big problem." It seemed a kind of treason to serve up these sacred songs to *paios,* profane consumers of pop music.

"It was tricky," Jeannot agrees. "Moïse's father, my

grandfather, my father, my brother are all pastors. We are right in the middle of this religion, deep inside. I am the only person in my family who is not baptised. I believe, but I don't practice." (Neither does Moïse, or any of the other musicians I talk to. "Practicing," which includes adult baptism, requires commitments not to drink or smoke or cheat on your spouse.) "We wanted to play this music in public, to non-Gypsies, but no one had ever done this. We would be the first."

Moïse explains, "I wanted to, but I didn't dare. I was ashamed to play our canticles to French people; I thought they would look down on them."

Tekameli went to the elders for permission. "We went to the patriarchs, like Tato's grandfather, as a matter of respect," Jeannot explains. "Tato's grandfather is one of the only people alive who can speak Kalo—not just a word or two, but fluently. There are people who tell you they speak Kalo, but it's fake. Tato's grandfather is the only one, and he would rather die than give it away to others. He *could* not divulge it, even if he wanted to."

"We were cunning," smiles Moïse. "We got their permission to play songs from the *Assemblée,* but they could not allow us to sing 'La Novia.' We tricked them. We went ahead and recorded a 'Novia,' and then invited the council of Gypsy elders to hear it. Well, of course, once they'd heard it, they couldn't resist."

The rehearsal breaks up. I am leaving town for a couple of days, but ask if I can come back to another session: will they still be rehearsing on Friday?

Moïse and Jeannot look blank. Friday? What's Friday?

Today, I remind them, is Tuesday the 4th. Tomorrow is Wednesday the 5th. Will they be rehearsing on Friday the

7th? Again, I've stepped into the abyss, asked a dumb *paio* question. I get out my Filofax and show them the week-at-a-glance. Moïse and Jeannot assume the expression I myself probably get when someone tries to explain to me compound interest rates or the internal workings of a computer. They nod politely in the hopes I will soon shut up and go away. This day is Tuesday, that day is Friday. We work through the days of the week together. Finally, Jeannot seems to get the idea. *"Vendredi, vendredi, vendredi—divendres,"* he explains in Catalan to Moïse. Oh, *divendres,* fine, agreed, I'll come by the Maison on Friday the 7th.

But then there's a hitch. "No, no, that's no good," says Jeannot. "We're playing a wedding on the 9th."

It takes another ten minutes of calendar-study to make Jeannot acknowledge that the 7th and the 9th are two different days, by which time I finally accept that these two young men, educated in the excellent French public-school system of the late 1970s and '80s, really are functionally illiterate.

We shake hands. "Till Friday."

They walk me back to my car—an ancient, decrepit Renault 5. I was lent the car by a friend, and never bothered to change its "75" license plate. Seventy-five means central Paris.

Jeannot listens to its bronchial wheeze with skepticism. "You're planning to drive that thing all the way to Paris tonight?"

So this is how illiteracy operates, a question of strategic priorities and selective ignorance, of memorizing certain emblems crucial to daily survival. You can't read the calendar date 7, but you can identify the 75 on a license plate.

4

Of course, they weren't there on Friday.

That was pretty much the last Tekameli rehearsal I ever saw. I tried, regularly: I wanted to hear their raw voices, bare of the blandishments of guitar and percussion. I wanted to watch Salomon beat rhythm on Thierry's thigh, and Moïse chew Kevin's ear.

What I discovered was that though the musicians were extremely affable in that present moment, once I lost sight of them, there was no apparent continuity to grab hold of. They were as elusive, as liable to vanish, as if they still moved in caravans. "Gypsy time" was like one of those fairy tales where a thousand years in "our" world is a moment in fairyland, and vice versa.

I would call, but Moïse's telephone was cut off. I tried the cell phone, but it was broken. I showed up at the apartment: tough luck, they'd been rehearsing all week, but now they were finished. Trying to go along to a second Tekameli rehearsal, I began to feel like the tag-along pest whom the other kids contrive to leave behind.

Sometimes it seemed a sure bet. I'd talk to Moïse at noon, and he'd say, Meet me at Haut Vernet at 1:45, but at 1:45 and at two and three, no one was there, and the next time I'd find out that Salomon had had important papers to fill out, or Tato's son had been taken to the emergency ward with an asthma attack. After another last minute no-show, Diane explained that she and Moïse and the kids, along with thirty other family members, had driven to the hospital in Montpellier, where a thirty-four-year-old uncle of Moïse's was in a diabetic coma, a family crisis which meant that Tekameli would not be operational for the foreseeable future.

"You can't play music with a heavy heart," she points out, reproachfully.

Another season gets totalled because Jeannot is moving into his new apartment. For an entire two months, the band is dormant: they don't meet, don't rehearse, don't play, because Jeannot has to move. You can't play music with a moving heart, apparently.

Along the way, I notice that the Gypsies' vague grasp of time and place is not only a way of escaping importunate non-Gypsies. Quite frequently, Moïse or Diane are prevented from realizing a cherished scheme by some failure of elementary logic. It's New Year's Day, and Moïse is taking off for Barcelona—one of the sprees from which he, his uncles, cousins, and nephews totter home three days later, red-eyed, with holes in their pockets and clashing alibis. But first he's got to raise the scratch, and Guy Bertrand (in Diane and Moïse's heated Gitan discussions of Guy Bertrand, the words "money" and *"paio"* recur obsessively) has refused.

"You tell him, Fernande."

Tell him what?

"He's going over to ASSEDIC [the unemployment agency] to get some money. I keep telling him the office will be closed, but he won't believe me."

"Moïse, it's New Year's Day. It's a national holiday. Offices are closed."

He doesn't believe me. If such an assertion is pure meanness on Diane's part, it's pig-ignorance on mine. Why would an office be closed when he needs it to be open?

5

It's a Ramadan lunchtime, and Guy Bertrand is eating couscous in a noisy Moroccan restaurant full of French busi-
nessmen who don't know or don't care that it's never a
good idea to eat in a restaurant whose entire staff is fasting.
The couscous restaurant's on a commercial boulevard opposite Guy Bertrand's accountant's office, in which he is due
very shortly, although maybe, he suggests, I can wait for him
outside.

Guy Bertrand is a busy man, perpetually rushing between
appointments with bank managers and lawyers, rehearsals in
Montpellier and Paris, performances in Toulouse, Lyons, Lille.
He is an owlish man, dark, slightly cross-eyed. That he dresses
in black and wears a ponytail does nothing to diminish his air
of bureaucratic fussiness.

Guy Bertrand is a Protestant from the southwest—like
Jeannot, he comes from a family of pastors. His family, however, are not fairground charismatics, but the kind of old-
line Protestants who went to the stake for their faith after
Louis XIV's revocation of the Edict of Nantes, and who in
France have a reputation for an austere probity that gets
up people's noses. ("I told you the French would never elect
a Protestant," a friend reminds me, when Prime Minister
Jospin comes third in the 2002 presidential elections.)

Guy Bertrand's line on everything is that pretty much
nothing exists until he finds it or creates it, and that as soon
as he moves on, it dissolves, and that everyone but he is an
asshole. Guy Bertrand is mightily sick of Gypsies and of Perpignan, and maybe he's right.

Bertrand is a clarinetist who also specializes in Mediterranean instruments such as the tabor and the hurdy-gurdy. In 1989, he left a job in Toulouse to become professor of traditional music at the Conservatoire National Regionale of Languedoc-Roussillon. By "traditional," the director of the conservatory meant Catalan *coblas*.

Bertrand arrived in Perpignan, bought himself a house by the conservatory, which is in St. Mathieu, a neighborhood part Gypsy, part North African, part illegal immigrant, part drug-dealer, and straightaway saw that the best "tradition" going was Gypsy.

"At the time, there was actually very little in the way of Gypsy music. There were groups that formed and disbanded every day. There was sacred music, there was wedding music, both of which were forbidden to be played outside the religious context (which is patently absurd, since the first thing a Gypsy does on meeting you is ask you to a wedding) and that was it."

"When I entered this community, I was in a privileged position," Bertrand explains. "I wasn't a politician, I wasn't a social worker, I wasn't a policeman, I was a musician. I began by approaching the old people, because that's where you must begin. They have traditions, they have capacities and talents that are dormant, they have respect (because respect for elders is still central to Gypsy culture), and they will lead you to the young."

"Tekameli is my invention; I wrote their music. There is talent, but no direction. When they themselves try to compose, the result is *'Au Clair de la Lune.'* I discovered the *Assembleés*—nobody knew them, nobody went there. Today, it's degraded, it's karaoke, it's a horror. I put together the Sony deal, I found them [Algerian rai star] Khaled, I brought them [Barcelona rumba star] Parrita."

Guy Bertrand founded the Casa Musicale, as well as setting up an adult literacy program at the conservatory for Moïse and other Gypsy musicians.

I ask him the question that haunts every discussion of Tekameli. A local reporter has just published a peculiarly malicious article claiming that the band is washed up and the Sony deal dead, because Tekameli has been unable to produce the contracted second album. Is it true that Tekameli is on the verge of breaking up?

Guy Bertrand puffs out his cheeks and shrugs.

He's left his accountant's office, and is giving me a ride back downtown. We pass the Place Cassanyes, where Gypsy garbagemen in fluorescent green are hosing down the sidewalks from the morning's market. Men in black suits hang out of battered cars. We pass a woman in a green-and-gold velvet kaftan who is carrying a basket containing a plucked chicken. I think, This place is godforsaken, but its broken beauties are in my bloodstream.

"It's not easy to work with Gypsies," Guy Bertrand observes. "They have difficult pasts, uncertain education, enormous family problems. At five or six years old, they're adorable, but they're running around in cafés all night. Very young, they fizzle out because they have no structure in their lives, no discipline, no vision, and hence they can't critique themselves, they can't develop. Musically, they are as good at fourteen as they ever will be.

"Have you heard Moïse sing recently? No? I'm not surprised. I have recordings of him from ten years ago that would make you cry. Moïse gets all the attention because he's got a pretty face, but he's ruined his voice. In all the years I've known him, Moïse has never done a single thing to deepen or improve or develop his music. All he's done is strut around for journalists, blowing his money, and making babies all over the world."

I ask Bertrand if he considers that there is much overt racism against Gypsies here.

Guy Bertrand sighs. "A group of Gypsies go out to a restaurant in Perpignan. They order a big meal and when they're done, they run away laughing, without paying the bill." He looks at me through owlish spectacles, as if to say, Would *you* welcome such clients in your restaurant?

"They live in a parallel society, operating a parallel economy, whose relation to ours is . . . bizarre. Gypsies and municipal politics—well, that's a bombshell I prefer not to discuss. Let's just say, they play the state very skillfully, they are slyer than you might imagine. You needn't be sorry for these Gypsies, they have more money than you or I will ever see."

Chapter Seven

1

Somewhere along the way, I am forced to acknowledge that Tekameli and I don't have much of a future. The world of Perpignan Gypsy music is a male world. Men and women who are not related by blood or marriage don't cross, at least not in daylight.

Occasionally, I meet Frenchwomen who are musicians themselves and who hang out with Gypsy musicians. There is Sara, who plays the guitar and is the only non-Gypsy I know who speaks Gitan, and Caro, who is a violinist in Kaloomé, the new group formed by Tato Garcia. But everybody knows that Tato has left his wife for Caro and that Sara had a romance with Moïse's brother Salomon, among other Gypsy husbands (since the men marry at seventeen, you're unlikely to meet a bachelor), and neither woman, understandably, is much welcome at home. And home is the heart of St. Jacques Gypsy-life—not rehearsals, not gigs. Anything worth knowing happens around the kitchen table.

Moïse is an old-fashioned Gypsy, and besides, he's shy. He can sleep with a woman, but he can't talk to one. Moïse doesn't mind having me around, over the years he even gets quite fond of me, but for a long time, there's a barrier that comes precisely from my being not just a *paia* but a journalist. That is, a person paid to ask prying questions. Understandably, most of what Moïse tells me, in answer to my questions, has an unquantifiable approximation to what a reporter might think of as the facts.

The Belgian writer Jan Yoors, who was raised by nomadic Gypsies as an adopted son, maintains that "the Gypsies have protected their cultural continuity behind an elaborate system of protective screens, so that reality is often the exact opposite of appearance. . . . When approached directly, they show a total disregard for consistency and may become totally incomprehensible about any matter they do not wish to discuss, without any sense of embarrassment on their part. They scorn the gullible *gadje* who are naive enough to believe that truthful answers can be obtained in such an unsubtle fashion."

Sometimes, by chance, I glimpse an alternative reality.

"Why did you drop out of Tekameli?" I ask Moïse's uncle Jérôme.

"I prefer to be at home, *tranquille*," says Jérôme.

"He got too scared of airplanes; he couldn't go on tour anymore," translates Moïse.

"And you, how do you feel about airplanes?"

"Me? Fine," says Moïse. "No problem."

The next day, Garth and his wife, Pascale, come over to our house for Sunday lunch. You won't believe the latest Tekameli drama, Pascale tells me. The week before, her brother, Guy Bertrand, was awoken by a phone call. It's Moïse—he's in police custody in Barcelona. That afternoon, Tekameli was supposed to fly from Barcelona to Lisbon for a concert. The other band members boarded the plane without a hitch, but Moïse had suddenly found himself absolutely incapacitated by his fear of flying. Fine, he'd thought, I'll sell my airplane ticket and take a bus. So there Moïse had stood, trying to flog his ticket to prospective passengers, but since he had neither passport, credit card, nor proof of purchase, the airport police had arrested him.

When I hear this story, which occurred a week before Moïse assured me he loves to fly, I figure I will only get to know Moïse by accident or proxy.

Moïse, on the other hand, takes an instant liking to my husband, whom he welcomes with relief as a sane and trustworthy man. If I want to find out what's going on with Tekameli, I ask Alastair to ask Moïse.

2

Almost unconsciously, I take another path. I stop by the apartment in the afternoons, when the women are alone. The second time I ring the buzzer of the apartment above La Fantaisie, I bring along my son, Theodore, a handsome, headstrong two-year-old who is crazy about guns, knives, and motorcycles, and who, at this tender age, exudes a swaggering outsized masculinity that people accustomed to simpler sexual codes find reassuring.

It's a wager—a way of disarming myself, of making myself less of a Martian to the Gypsies, for whom a woman without visible children is a freak of nature—and it works. Kevin teaches Theodore martial-arts kicks and leads him off into his bedroom to watch Pokemon videos. Diane tells him that she too is a motorcycle-fiend, and we plan a trip to the motocross track.

The next time, I bring my daughter, Maud. Diane praises her beauty, feeds her candy. She gets in the habit of buying my children presents attentively attuned to their current passions— a toy knife for Theodore, a mask and snorkel for Maud.

Every week now, I drop by the apartment for a cup of coffee, sometimes with the children, or with a friend, sometimes on my own.

Moïse is mostly out. When he's in town, he spends his afternoons at Le Rugbyman, a bar near the fairground, playing cards with Jeannot or with Diane's brother Samir. Often he's away on tour—performing in the north of France, or in Spain, or Italy, or Belgium. ("Tekameli's tours, it's like the Gypsies' old voyagings," remarks Jeannot. "We are always on the road—a little money here, a little money there, then home, *tranquille.*")

When Moïse is home, you can find the three of them— Moïse in black suit and gold crucifix, Diane in silk pajamas, Kevin in boxer shorts—sitting at the kitchen table, playing gin rummy with two packs, while Baby Marlon squawks in his playpen. They play cards, we chat, we listen to music, Diane and Moïse fight about money and cigarettes. Moïse is a bit of a skinflint, a bit of a tease, and he likes to keep money back from Diane, he likes to withhold cigarettes.

Diane and I drink cold coffee and smoke red Marlboros. Diane takes me into their bedroom to show me videos of Tekameli concerts, of Kevin's full-contact tournaments, of family Christmases at Jérôme's house. I ask who's who, and thereby gain accidental insights.

"That's Miriam," Diane explains, identifying a gawky adolescent, hanging back as the other women urge her to dance. "She's Moïse's daughter. You didn't know Moïse has a daughter?"

I have been told by then that Moïse has *many* daughters, but I didn't know Diane knew.

Moïse's daughter Miriam is thirteen years old. Moïse had her when he was fifteen. The girl's mother went on to have a bunch more children, none of whom she was in any condition to raise herself, and died of AIDS a few years ago.

"I heard that Miriam was going to be taken into foster care. I said, No *way* is Moïse's daughter going into care. She came to live with us when Kevin was a baby; I brought her up as my own child. She *is* my child."

Miriam has just moved in with her grandfather, because she's engaged to be married, and she wants to be closer to her betrothed, who lives next door.

"She's going to be married at thirteen?"

Diane looks at me pityingly. Of course not, stupid. She's going to be married *next year,* when she's *fourteen.*

"Hey, Mo," she calls to her husband. "Fernande didn't know you had a daughter."

"No?" says Moïse, suavely apologetic. "A little adventure of my youth."

Often Diane and I go out for a jaunt. Diane is a passionate spendthrift, and what she loves (and I hate) is to cruise the malls along the highway to Spain. There's always a pretext: her new stilettos are too tight; she's broken the tall blue vase for her artificial flowers; Marlon needs summer clothes.

On the way, we drop by her sister Linda's apartment, and Linda's fifteen-year-old daughter, Tanya, joins us. We wander over to the rue des Carmes to pick up Kevin and Marlon from Granny Antoinette's. We stop to chat to Aunt Jeanne, to Uncle Jérôme, to the cousins who are sitting in the sun.

Before long, I've been semi-adopted by Diane and her family, bundled into the cozy scolding beehive of this crumbling Mediterranean slum, in which the developed world's notions of public and private, of urban and rural, of child and adult, have scant meaning, in which roosters live in the kitchen, and six-year-olds are still pushed in strollers, but smoke cigarettes and go to midnight movies, and any unfamiliar car tooling down your street is scrutinized as if it might be carrying suicide-bombers.

Once only in St. Jacques does someone ask why I'm there. He is a short, square man in a black suit and a white shirt. It's Pitou Cargol, the "mediator," who when he's told I'm Diane's friend, lays his hand on his heart and tells me we're all God's children, Gypsy, French, green, purple.

"I hate him," says Diane, afterward. "He preaches education, and his kids can't read because he never let them go to school."

3

The Gypsies think I'm a laugh. They find me naïve, touchingly simple, a person who comes from the toughest city in the world and who yet appears ignorant of the most basic rules of self-preservation, who comes from the center of world fashion and yet dresses like a handyman. Antoinette, when I tell her that I've just come from the hairdresser, suggests that I should get my money back: the woman's cut it all crooked!

Diane loves to tell the story of how we first met, when I came into her apartment announcing that I was "crazy about Tekameli," and how wherever I go—no matter into what potential den of thieves I've entered—I immediately throw my pocketbook into a corner (she mimics), and forget about it. You have to watch out for Gypsies, she warns. Even Jérôme, visiting his own nephew's apartment, will sometimes slip a little something into his pocket, almost unknowing.

Diane knows people who have money, such as Nicole, the doctor's widow, whom Diane praises for her "simplicity," but my own simplicity is more convoluted. She sees all the indicators of money—our regular family trips to New York or London—but she can't believe we're rich, because if she were rich, she wouldn't wear flea-market clothes and drive a tin lizzie. When my daughter, Maud, presses her nose longingly to the window of a store selling lurid Chinese bric-a-brac, Diane tells her fondly, "If you got those sorts of tastes, sweetheart, you'll have to marry a millionaire."

Diane and Linda and their mother find me just as remiss about my children as my handbag. How can I entrust them to a babysitter? They would never let anybody outside the family mind their children. Linda, in a touching reversal of old legends about Gypsy child-stealers, is convinced if she doesn't hang on tight to her son in public parks, some white French person's going to snatch him.

The Gypsy women think it's wild that I sometimes show up at the house with men I'm not married to. Afterward, they rate my friends' looks, swooning with pantomime lust over the gorgeousness of a young artist I introduce them to. Linda and Diane are horrified when I tell them that he's married to an older woman.

"If he were a Gypsy, his mother would pick him the choicest fifteen-year-old virgin," says Linda. "Is his wife beautiful?"

"Not especially."

"Well, then, she must be *very, very* rich."

4

Diane hates Gypsies. Linda hates Gypsies. Even Moïse, who is an out-and-out Gypsy to the core, claims to hate Gypsies. Above all, they hate the Gypsies of St. Jacques. Why?

"They are hypocrites," says Diane. "They are vicious," says Linda. "I have known all sorts of people, and all sorts of Gypsies, and I think I can honestly say that the Gypsies of St. Jacques are peculiarly perverse."

Diane and Linda explain to me *la loi gitane,* according to St. Jacques. Women may not leave the house without their husbands' permission. They are not supposed to drive cars, smoke cigarettes, or drink alcohol. They may not wear skirts above the ankle or trousers. They are not allowed to go to restaurants or cafés, to engage in sports or hold jobs where they might encounter men.

All they are allowed to do, in fact, is stay at home, covered in head-to-toe black, scrubbing floors, cooking, waiting on the men, and making sure their daughters are never seen talking to a boy.

The only permitted conduit to the outside world, the only source of licit entertainment, besides television or trips to the doctor, is the *Assemblée,* where they get to sit and watch their menfolk testify to spiritual awakenings of which women are deemed incapable. (Indeed, you could say that St. Jacques's switch from Catholicism to an in-house Pentacostalism has narrowed Gypsy women's horizons even further.)

How Gypsy women in fact manage is sometimes by following the letter of the law—their skirts are ankle length, but they're made of clinging Lurex and slit to the thigh—and sometimes by the doubleness otherwise characteristic of life in Riyadh or Tehran. They smoke and drink, but only at home when there's no one to squeal on them; they go to the movies, but only in *paio* neighborhoods where they won't be seen. Diane and Linda keep jeans and sneakers at their aunt's house in Paris: as soon as they get off the train, they become free women.

One sunny afternoon, I take Linda and her son Mickaël to the park at Moulin-à-Vent. At the stoplight, we pull up beside a car full of Gypsy teenagers. By St. Jacques demographics, we are the age of these boys' grandmothers, they can see Mickaël in the backseat, but they nonetheless lean out the window and make salacious remarks.

"They do that because they see I'm with a *paia*," Linda explains. "In St. Jacques mentality, you can only be with a *paia* for one reason, to whore around."

"Here, if a woman so much as wears sunglasses or trousers, they will brush up against her, they'll touch her ass, they'll say, Nice butt, then—mocking—Oh, I mistook you for a *paia*. Have you noticed that St. Jacques women only carry plastic bags? If a woman has a handbag, they're up in arms. Now she thinks she's French! They can't understand that Frenchwomen have such freedom and *yet* they behave themselves, they are correct. It makes no sense to these Gypsies, because if *they* had the same freedom, they know what they would do with it."

In St. Jacques marriages, misery and violence seem to be taken for granted. I hear too many stories of husbands' routinely beating up their wives, of an ethic in which rape is considered more manly than making love, because a wife's "enjoying it" means she's a whore.

A Frenchwoman whose daughter married a musician from NG San Jaume (the groom, at seventeen, was already twice divorced) tells me, "I got tired of seeing my girl with black eyes, swollen lips, bruises. He would rather hit her than say hello. When I took her and their little boy back home with me, he and his friends came and smashed my car. Another time they threw a fire bomb into the living room. In the end, I had to get a police injunction against him."

It's a measure of Gypsy oppressiveness that the growing number of St. Jacques wives who've run off with Muslim neighbors describe their wonder at how open-minded a man can be. I ask Linda, whose last boyfriend was a Turkish Kurd and the father of her son Mickaël, whether she thinks it's true that Muslim wives are better off than Gypsies.

"Without a doubt," she replies. "Just think of the wedding. In an Arab wedding, there is the marriage sheet that must be produced, but at least it's the bride and groom who go off alone to the bedroom. If she's not pure, they can concoct a way out together. For Gypsies, it's a nasty old woman who is paid to penetrate the girl, like a gynecologist but with dirty hands, in front of all the husband's family. It's terrifying, it's inhuman. What kind of introduction is that to conjugal love?"

5

Diane keeps the door to her apartment locked and bolted.

Because Linda and her children live upstairs, and because of the communal nature of Gypsy day-to-day, there is a steady flux in and out of the apartment, but each time someone leaves—even if it's only her nephew Mickaël who wants to retrieve his Power Ranger toys from upstairs, or Kevin who's running downstairs to hand his father a video to return to the store—she double-locks the door afterward, and shoves a bolster against it.

I never learn what Diane's afraid of. Somebody tells me, "Moïse Espinas's family is not very popular. It's not unlikely that someday someone will come and break his door down."

The apartment would be bright and airy—Diane is a fanatical cleaner—except that the midnight-blue curtains are permanently drawn, the shutters half-closed, so it remains in total darkness. The apartment gets on her nerves: a corner of the wallpaper's peeled away, and some floor tiles are discolored from a leak the landlord never gets around to fixing.

Over the years, Diane continuously complains to me that the landlord hasn't yet replaced the wallpaper or the tiles. When he does, she will buy new living-room furniture, even though what she's got is already new. She would prefer a blue sofa and armchairs to yellow ones. She believes that if she can only get the landlord to do these minor repairs, her luck will have changed, and she will no longer be quite so unhappy. When he eventually does fix the leak and repair the tiles, Diane buys the midnight-blue furniture set, but soon she wants to change it for lavender furniture and curtains. If the curtains were lavender, she'd be really happy. And yet, her glooms can lift at a trifle. Put on music she likes, and she's dancing, laughing, black eyes sparkling.

The apartment is her prison. She shuffles back and forth, back and forth, smoking, bolting coffee, chewing the fleshy nubs that are all that remain of her nails. She swallows pills, she summons the doctor, she has stomachaches, chest pains, bouts of bronchitis. She's perpetually inhaling her asthma spray, or crouched over the humidifier or even a wheeled oxygen tank. She takes so many pills she can't wake up to open the door.

Diane's life is a permanent medical emergency, in which illness provides the sole excitement. If it's not Diane, it's Moïse who out of the blue has fallen into a coma which may be epilepsy, but which even the experts cannot explain. If it's not Moïse, it's Baby Marlon, who has eczema, bronchitis, chronic diarrhea, or Kevin, whose asthma is so bad he spent most of his early life in the emergency room.

"When he was two, he had lung disease," Diane says. "We took him to doctors all over France. At the hospital in Montpellier, they told me he would die. I punched the doctor in the face. Kevin was on an IV. I said, Unplug him. I had him driven by ambulance back to Perpignan to be treated by a pastor at the *Assemblée,* who laid on hands. The next day, I took Kevin back to the hospital, the doctor said he was cured. There wasn't the slightest trace on his lungs."

Another time, she asks me to come over because she and Moïse have split up. "It's over; I've left him. Do you think it's normal for a man to hit his wife in the street?"

(Well, if he's a St. Jacques Gypsy, the street's the best place to hit her, just so everyone can see he's a real man.) "What happened?" I asked.

"I refused to have his brother Salomon's wife, Maza, in the house, so he hit me."

"Why wouldn't you have her over?"

"She was telling everybody she had tuberculosis. Would *you* have someone in your house with tuberculosis? I said, I don't want her infecting my children. Isn't that normal?"

"Does she really have tuberculosis?"

"She was going around saying she does. Now she says she doesn't."

Diane is sitting in her pajamas in the dark. Sick, as usual.

Depressed. *Fatiguée, fatiguée.* "We are dust," she informs me. "We begin as dust, we end as dust. Why create more suffering in the world?

"Maza said to me, I'm going to get my father and my brothers to beat you up. I told her, So what? I'm going to get *my* father and *my* brothers to beat up your father and your brothers, and meanwhile, Moïse's father's telling me, Out of my house, whore!"

I ask Diane about Salomon and Maza's first child, who was brain-damaged and died.

"The child used to have seizures," Diane told me. "She'd cry and cry, and Maza would hit her to stop her crying. I'd say, Maza, stop, there's something not right with that child; she's genuinely in pain, but Maza didn't understand."

"After her funeral, Salomon and Maza went out to a Quick"—a sub-McDonald's burger chain—"and ordered waffles with whipped cream. Is that normal? You or I, we'd want to die alongside the child, but Salomon and Maza, they had three more kids, boom-boom-boom, and they never mention her, never go to her grave."

Diane's ailments are as mystifying as Maza's: she might have to have an operation to remove the "mushrooms" in her stomach, or a clot in her lungs, or to straighten a twisted kidney or fix a herniated disk. When I first meet Diane, she's thin for the mother of a nine-month-old baby, but later she swells up because of the steroids she's on. She has heavy black circles under her hooded eyes, and the spooky effect is compounded by her changing hair colors and hairstyles: sometimes layered Old Gold shag, sometimes orange African braids. She's tiny, and wears platform shoes so she doesn't "disappear."

But when she's happy, she's got this tough, broken-nosed beauty, the sweet, wiry pluck of a girl-boxer.

"You know how you meet me," says her sister Linda, "and I seem so bright and friendly, and Diane seems like a nut? But the truth is it's Diane who's all heart; she'll give you the clothes off her back. And me, I don't trust *anybody*."

It's true about Diane. Every time I find myself exasperated beyond endurance, she wins me back with her rough warm generosity, her live sense of other people's pain.

"She's depressive," continues Linda. "And who wouldn't be, living the way she does? I tell her, 'Cut the pills, get out of the house, go to a gym, take some courses. You've got a nice husband who looks after the children, and doesn't mind if you go out.' But she won't."

I find myself dispatching similar bromides, observing to Diane that if she wants to cure her stomachaches, varying a diet of black coffee, pills, and cigarettes might be more to the point than surgery.

Diane watches her son, home from school and on his way to soccer practice, grab cookies from the kitchen cabinet. "He's bulimic," she says, irritably. "You're bulimic, you know what, Kevin, you're bulimic, stuffing your face all the time."

Kevin smiles politely. He's a quick kid. When women talk, he's learned, you don't listen, you just nod agreeably, until they go too far and you need to throw a tantrum, just to draw the line.

Diane watches Moïse cook himself supper at four p.m.—a plate of sardines, toast, a hamburger peeled from a stack of individually wrapped sheets of processed meat and fried till it's an even gray throughout. Moïse is considered a good husband because he doesn't expect Diane to cook his meals, because it's he who feeds the baby—directly from the baby-food jar. Moïse slices a tomato, hunts for vinegar in vain.

"Why don't you use the dressing I bought?" Diane demands. "He's fussy," she says to me. "He doesn't like bottled dressing, he wants it 'homemade.' "

The moment Moïse has cooked his meal and sits down to eat, Diane jumps up and grabs me by the arm, dragging me to the door. "Come on, let's go."

I hesitate, finding it disturbingly barbaric to walk out on someone who's just sat down to eat, then follow.

In her more optimistic moments, Diane thinks I can help her escape, because I have a car and spending money and because I like her, and our friendship soon devolves into a teasing tug-of-war between what she wants, which is to cruise shopping malls and discos, and what I want, which is to hear stories about Gypsy lives.

And yet, those days when I do allow myself to be kidnapped by Diane, when we hang out at the Racing Bull Sports Club, the martial-arts gym where Kevin does his full-contact training, or drive way too fast alongside the railroad tracks paralleling the Route d'Espagne, when we surf the malls, bumming cigarettes, sassing shop assistants, blasting salsa, it's a kind of wild abandoned fun I haven't known since I was seventeen.

And in the intervals between malls and martial arts, I hear the stories I'm waiting for.

Chapter Eight

1

It's Sunday afternoon, the day of Diane's pizza lunch party.

After the other guests have left, Diane and Linda and I settle down in Linda's upstairs apartment. Linda rocks her nephew Marlon to sleep in her arms.

The glittery March sunlight streams through Linda's window; she puts a covering over the sleeping child's head to keep the light from his eyes, and the conversation begins.

It is I who ask the questions, and Linda who answers, because they happen to be questions she's spent a lifetime thinking over. The story she tells me—with gruff, muttered additions from Diane—is the story of what brought their family to Paris, and what brought them back again to the confines of St. Jacques, about the compromises each of Antoinette's four children made between Gypsyness and assimilation, between the modern world and tribal loyalty.

Their mother, Antoinette, was born in St. Jacques, right after the war. All her life, she knew she wanted to escape.

121

The Gypsy code of honor, its promise that the family and neighborhood will protect you, had failed her, and laid her open in turn to wider possibilities.

"Our grandfather was a market seller who was 'touched' by the hand of God, and became a pastor," says Linda. "He traveled all over preaching among the Gypsies: he founded one of the first churches here in Roussillon. He was Josep Caragol."

Josep Caragol ran off with a *paia*, leaving his wife and six children. His wife, in turn, went to live with another man, leaving the children with their grandmother, who was too frail to look after them.

Antoinette, at sixteen, went out to work to support her younger brothers and sisters. She found a job in the Bella doll factory, on the outskirts of Perpignan. Bella, founded in the 1920s, was a great French Catalan institution. The dolls were world famous, their dresses were made of real lace. Young people today speak with nostalgic pride of their parents' or grandparents' jobs at the Bella factory—a paternalistic place that provided a home for its workers. (Jeannot, Tekameli's bassist, tells me of his grandfather, a painter at Bella, who invented a secret recipe for flesh color which dollmakers around the world tried in vain to extract from him.)

At Bella, Antoinette for the first time met non-Gypsies. Her best friend was a Portuguese girl from Toulouse. When her friend quit the factory and moved to Paris, Antoinette was determined to follow her.

It was the late '60s; the world was exploding. "You watched TV," explains her daughter Linda, "and you saw there was this *life* out there, where women could go to college, work in offices, have boyfriends. In St. Jacques, even to buy a loaf of bread, you needed a grandmother to go with you. The pressure of rumor, of gossip, the importance of reputation and virginity was such that if you were caught talking to a boy, it was marriage. Our aunt—they found her photograph in a boy's room, she had to marry him."

"What happens in such a marriage?" I ask.

"You learn to love someone afterward," says Linda, philosophically. "You live together, you get used to each other. There's always something to love."

Antoinette had a favorite cousin, with whom she had long been scheming to run away to Paris, but her cousin got married to a Frenchman. Later, Linda tells me the sad end to this story. The couple, after many years in Italy, move back to St. Jacques, but their daughter, who had fallen in love with a Turk who married her in order to get his papers and then dumped her, is persecuted by neighborhood Gypsies. She tries to maintain what she considers a normal life, but whenever she leaves the house, women scream, Whore! Boys brush up against her ass. In desperation, she finally marries a Gypsy—from a low-caste family, since she's used goods—and takes refuge in the St. Jacques equivalent of the headscarf.

Antoinette was determined not to get press-ganged into a Gypsy marriage. She delayed and delayed, Penelope-like, astonishingly late—till she was twenty-one. Then, having reached her majority, she took off for Paris, to join her Portuguese girlfriend.

"Her father and uncles came to bring her back, but she had waited on purpose till she was legally free," Linda says.

The two girls shared a studio in the nineteenth arrondissement. Every day, Antoinette canvassed the employment agencies, answered ads in newspapers. Within a week, she had found herself a job as a waitress in a restaurant called the Baobab.

I have seen photographs of Antoinette from her early Paris days. It's 1970: she has black-crayoned eyebrows, a full figure, a brooding, sensual, operatic style. One of the Baobab's regular customers took a fancy to her.

"A Guinean who drove a white Porsche—sounds like a pimp, no?" reflects Linda. "But Mama says he worked at the Embassy."

Antoinette got pregnant by her Guinean "fiancé." Only then did he tell her he had a French wife at home.

There was a quieter customer from the Baobab who had always had his eye on Antoinette. He was a Algerian Berber named Tony Meziani. He was her age—twenty-two—and, like Antoinette, he was a worker. Already, he had a good job as a railway controller. They got married, and six months later, Linda was born.

"All my life, I've asked my mother why I looked so different from my sister and brothers, why I *felt* so different. It's only very recently that she told me the truth, that my real father was African. Suddenly everything made sense, why I've always had this black thing—for black music, for black people, black culture."

The unknown Guinean must have been a beauty, for Linda is tall and queenly, with big smoldering eyes, a drop-dead figure she knows how to carry, and a combination of sexual fire and formidable dignity.

"I don't know how much Tony's ever wanted to admit. As far as he's concerned, I'm his daughter."

Tony Meziani is a complicated man—sensitive, melancholy, eager to be loved—a drinker, says Linda. In his own house, or at family gatherings, he strikes one as painfully isolated. (Linda says his own friends are Spanish, Sicilian, Portuguese, people with whom—unlike Gypsies—he can talk

current affairs, but "no Arabs.") You see in him an intro-
vertedness, a feeling of inadequacy, the same depression that
afflicts Diane and that would make alcohol a temptation.

Tony had left Algeria when he was sixteen, and although
he wasn't religious, he had "retained in some ways the mentality of *Là-bas* (Over There)," Linda explains. "My parents
love each other very much, and he gave up everything for my
mother. When he saw that his parents didn't accept her, he
cut off his own family for her sake. Still, in thirty years, I've
never seen my parents kiss. If there was a kiss on television,
everyone had to turn their heads. For us girls, there were no
boys, no birthday parties. Of course, that made me all the
more curious."

Tony and Antoinette opened a restaurant together in the
eleventh arrondissement. It prospered, and they opened a
second restaurant in the thirteenth. They had four children
in six years: Linda, Diane, and two younger boys, Samir and
Daniel.

The family lived in a project on the outskirts of Paris.
Because Tony and Antoinette worked day and night, Linda,
the eldest child, became "the little mother with the apartment key around her neck," who kept house and raised the
younger children.

"Cinderella?" I inquire.

"Not really, we had plenty of money, we wanted for
nothing," Linda says.

"Our father wanted to move us to a nice villa with a garden," Diane interjects. "But we children howled. Don't leave
us at home with a housekeeper and a dog! We wanted to stay
with our friends in the project. He said, These kids are nuts!"

Linda, in particular, had a reason for not wanting
to move. Linda was friends with the boy from downstairs,

a handsome, sassy kid, half-Caribbean, half-French, called Mario.

Linda was the "perfect little grown-up": dedicated, responsible, a straight-A student. But she also had a vivid sexual curiosity, intensified, she believes, by her parents' prudishness. When she was thirteen and Mario was sixteen, they started fooling around. She liked it, and they continued. Two years later, Linda got pregnant.

"My father flipped. He expected trouble from Diane, but from me, never. What hit my father the worst was the boy was black. Today I wonder if it gave him an uncomfortable flashback to his wife's having a baby by a black man."

Tony put the family restaurants up for sale, and announced that they were moving to his wife's hometown of Perpignan. Linda was sent on ahead to stay with her aunt Jeanne and uncle Francisquet in the rue des Carmes.

"I gave birth all by myself in the Perpignan hospital," an infamously ghoulish institution. "It was a terrifying experience that still gives me nightmares."

Linda, the model child, had disgraced herself and ruined her family's big-city success story. She had always assumed she would go on to college, pursue a career. Now she was a teen mother, marooned in a hidebound provincial town of whose mores she realized she'd been ignorant.

"Until we moved here, I never even knew we were Gypsies. Of course, there was this special language that my mother spoke with her sisters and that I picked up quickly, when we came here on holidays, but to me, we were no different from our Paris schoolfriends. Once we moved back to Perpignan, everything changed. Aunt Jeanne was now always warning me, Don't do this, don't do that, watch who you speak to. People were saying, But how could she have had a baby when she's not married? Here I saw that women weren't allowed to leave the house without their husband's permission, that everybody was always spying to catch you out."

Tony and Antoinette took over a bar-restaurant by the train station. "Every night there were knife fights, thugs emptying the cash register. And my father, who was innocent and liked everybody at first, didn't understand about Gypsies. He nearly went bust giving our drunken uncles credit."

The children were now old enough to work in their parents' bar: Diane, who dropped out of school in the fifth grade, speaks fondly of her experiences as a waitress. She holds up her slash-scarred wrists to show me how you balance three full plates of food on one arm. "I did the night shift; it was a rackety life. I had nowhere to sleep in the day, because Samir was blasting his music."

Linda tried to finish high school, but found herself exhausted by the demands of a baby. Meanwhile, she and Mario pursued their love in secret. He came down to Perpignan to see her; Tony, when he found out, threatened to have the boy arrested for statutory rape.

"Mario waited for me. He was determined for us to be together. Before he went off to do his military service, he came down to see me once more. I was now nineteen. He said, 'The only way I can keep you is to make you another baby.' (He was crazy about our daughter, Tanya.) 'I'm going to make you another baby so we can be together.' "

Mario went into the army, and Linda found that she was indeed pregnant. "I realized I couldn't face going through all that mess with my father again, so I sneaked off for an abortion. But Mario somehow *knew* that it had 'worked.' He asked me and he asked me, and when I finally told him what I'd done, it broke his heart. He could not accept it."

Later, Mario had a son by another woman. And Linda, too, lived for a time with the Turkish Kurd by whom she had Mickaël, but neither relationship lasted.

"His family calls me 'Mario's wife.' What do you expect? I have known them all since I was a child. They are Tanya's family, and mine, too. I go stay with them in Paris; when Mario's sister gets a vacation, she comes to visit me here."

"Mario has done very well for himself. He started his own security agency. He and Tanya are extremely close; they spend every holiday together."

And meanwhile, Linda and Mario have never stopped being in love, this stubborn, unstoppable-ungoable love. Once or twice she's agreed to leave everything and go live with him, but something—usually in the shape of Mickaël's father threatening to kidnap Mickaël and take him back to Turkey—always intervenes.

"Just now Mario's learned I'm seeing someone new—a Frenchman—and for the first time ever, he's asked me to marry him."

"Why don't you?"

She reflects. "He's a man who loves women. Since he was a child. He loves-loves-loves-loves women. Too much. It's his thing. I'm scared. He tells me, But you're my favorite. I say, I don't want to be the favorite in your harem. He says, If I had you, I wouldn't need anybody else. But I don't believe it, he loves women too much."

"You've got tears in your eyes," Diane accuses me. It's true. And Diane understands why, for she, too, thinks her sister should marry Mario, who is "beautiful and fun and sexy and kind" and who has loved Linda since they were children, and whom Tanya too worships, for he is more attentive, more present than many fathers who live under the same roof as their children.

Linda laughs, but there's fear in her glance. She says, "You don't understand. It's become something crazy in our heads because it's unrealized, because we have known each other all our lives and yet we've never lived together. *C'est un amour des gamins.* I tell him, 'You're a grown man, you are the head of a company; I too have an adult life, but together, we become children again.' "

"I'll give you an example. When he first kissed me, I was thirteen and when he tried to put his tongue in my mouth, I was revolted, I gagged and said, Get that thing out of my mouth. And he didn't try again. Eighteen years later, he still won't kiss me on the mouth because he is afraid of disgusting me. Or—we don't undress in front of each other, we don't walk around naked, because before, I was shy. When I am with other men, I am an adult, I kiss, I'm naked, but with him, I'm still a child."

"You want to see Mario?" Linda asks me. She puts on a video from last Christmas in Paris, filmed in Tanya's Guadeloupean grandmother's apartment. Here is the record of Linda and Tanya's other life, their Parisian life, semi-secret, this place where they wear tight jeans and speak French and go out to nightclubs.

It makes an odd counterpart to Diane's home video of the same Christmas. At Diane's family Christmas, in Jérôme's house on the rue des Carmes, the women dance together in a zombied trance, while the men sit and drink. At Linda's Christmas, men and women are comfortably entwined. Here is Tanya, bebopping with Mario, who looks more like her boyfriend than her father, a tall, green-eyed young man with the smiling somnolent ease of a big cat.

"He's put on weight," remarks Linda, proprietarily.

At the end, you see Linda and Mario together, these once-and-future lovers rather self-consciously hip-to-hip, dancing slow, two people who've been through too much together and keep on telling themselves they don't stand a hope.

"He kept asking me, Is your heart beating fast? I can feel your heart jumping."

And was it?

She laughs, uncomfortably. "I told him, Dream on."

2

Linda is no church mouse. When people discuss her, it's words like "majestic" that tend to get used. She's a gorgeous woman in full command of her own sexuality. Her elegantly tailored clothes—charcoal-gray jersey with black fur trim, black patent-leather high-heel pumps—show off her full bust and hips, her long slim legs.

She likes to laugh, she loves to dance, she's crazy about music. When Diane wiggles to her favorite salsa band, Ketama, their mother says, contemptuously, "Sit down, child, you'll never have half your sister's class."

Yet by Gypsy standards, Linda's lot is dismal. She works as a secretary at the local high school. The pay's terrible, but at least she gets to keep the same hours and vacations as her children. "Gypsies tell me, You're out of your mind to work for six hundred dollars a month: you could get eight hundred on welfare."

Her scrimp-and-save ethic they find positively barbaric. Her cousins lambast her for not buying brand-name clothes and fancier toys for her children, and her neighbors reproach her for allowing her daughter to go on to high school. "The whole family came to me when Tanya was fifteen and said, Get her out of school, you are ruining her chances."

In the evenings, Linda stays home, helping Tanya with her homework, putting Mickaël to bed, studying for the national exam that will give her a better-paid position in the school system. It's hard to get Linda out of the house. You invite her to dinner, to a concert, but she's tired, she's got to get up early the next morning. You sometimes get the impression that the fierce self-control that enabled this teen mother to buck the St. Jacques spirit of lethargy and derision has frozen into overdrive. She can no longer let go.

And Linda's children reflect her discipline. Tanya, a lively, confident, grown-up teenager, intends to go on to the university in Montpellier to study literature and psychology. In the meantime, she's got her own hip-hop dance group. Five-year-old Mickaël, in a world in which boys are rewarded for being obstreperous, is docile and considerate. But even he sometimes objects to his mother's un-Gypsyish ways.

"When I stop him from grabbing cookies all day long like his cousins, he protests, *'Sem poos payoos.'* (We aren't *paios.*) When I try to get him to say 'Hello' or 'Goodbye' or 'Please' or 'Thank you,' *Sem poos payoos.* Gypsies aren't supposed to greet each other; why am I trying to make him into a freak? But I have no worries about Mickaël. He's a thoughtful boy, already he gets good grades. Yesterday, he asked me what 'consciousness' meant."

Linda is devout, she goes to an American-style Baptist gospel church, rather than the Gypsy *Assemblée,* and attends a Bible-study group. She wants to know which religion I am, and all about my family and upbringing, how Americans live and think, what kind of differences there are between rich and poor, men and women. She's the first person I've met in Roussillon who asks me back the kind of questions I ask her and thereby frees me from the discomfiting inequality of being a foreign journalist, the mean one-way-street of I-know-you-but-you-don't-know-me.

And I find myself talking to Linda about things I haven't told anyone in France, because no one else has been able to formulate the questions.

3

French people in Perpignan believe that Gypsies live in self-imposed quarantine, as if St. Jacques still had its ghetto walls. Gypsies, too, are anxious to perpetuate this image of steadfast endogamy, of *petit cousin* marrying *petite cousine* throughout generations. But in most Gypsy families, dig deeper and you find the old Mediterranean story of *métissage*. (Is Pascal a Gypsy? Of course he's a Gypsy, he can barely speak French. Why's he blond? His mother's French. Why does Mike have blue eyes? His father's Sicilian.)

Although *la loi gitane* appears to be Taliban-strict, what I am discovering is that in fact there are humanizing inconsistencies, numerous instances of prodigal children who are welcomed back into the fold.

Antoinette had her first child by a married African, and the others by an Algerian, but today she is a venerable matriarch. Linda at thirty-one is still unmarried though she has had one child by a French Guadeloupean and another by a

Turkish Kurd. She has a job, her own car, a French boyfriend (whom she sees on the sly), and she sends her daughter to a coed high school.

Occasionally, there's an outburst. Jérôme's wife, Sylvie, in a spat with Linda, calls her "a filthy black," her niece Maëva rouses a malicious titter among the adults when she asks how it can be that Aunt Linda "has had two men." Yet when you see Linda at large Gypsy gatherings, it is evident that she is regarded with an awe amounting to veneration.

"How did you get away with it?" I ask Linda. "When you were a teenager in St. Jacques, didn't boys treat you differently, knowing you'd already slept with somebody?"

"Never," Linda replies. "Everybody's always treated me with respect, because I obey the rules. If my aunt told me, You musn't do this, I didn't do it. I'm a chameleon. It's easy for me to exist in several worlds. With Mario's family, I speak a little Creole. Here, I wear long skirts, I don't smoke, my daughter doesn't go out with boys. In the office, nobody knows I'm a Gypsy, they assume I'm black or Arab. If they knew, they'd be terrified!"

Linda understood the rules of the game: you wear a long black skirt, and you do what you like underneath that skirt. Diane didn't get it.

"I was a tomboy," Diane says. "I was always looking for trouble. You should have seen me when we moved from Paris to St. Jacques. I had a boy's haircut, jeans, earring in one ear, I rode a motorcycle. I got kicked out of school for slugging the teacher, and never went back. A friend and me, we used to do little burglaries. We broke into people's homes, into a store . . ."

Linda tells me that Diane ran with a dangerous gang. Her best friend was a Gypsy girl who nowadays is a recluse so doped up she weighs two hundred and fifty pounds, stinks of piss, and doesn't recognize you.

People were scared that if Diane weren't taken in hand, she would go the same way.

"How did you meet Moïse?" I asked Diane.

"As I was always doing *bêtises,* he came to ask for me, and my mother said yes."

"No, Diane," Linda reproves her sister, "That's not how it was. In those days, Diane was often at our aunt Sylvie's house. And Moïse, who was separated from his first wife, used to come to see his uncle Jérôme. Jérôme and Sylvie planted the idea in our mother's head: Look, here is Diane, who doesn't listen to a word, who runs around the streets all night. Marry her to Moïse, before she gets the family in serious trouble."

Moïse at the time was hardly a catch. He had barely been to school, he'd already had a child by a junkie, and been picked up by the police for car theft.

"He was malleable," admits Linda. "But he was always a nice kid. He had no job, but he played the guitar in restaurants and at weddings with Jérôme."

Moïse went to Diane's house to ask for her hand in marriage. Antoinette was willing, but Tony wasn't. "He knew the Gypsy mentality, he didn't want his daughter with a husband who lay around the house all day and beat her up, but on the other hand he saw the trouble Diane was getting into, so he was forced."

When they were seventeen years old, Diane and Moïse got married—not in a real Gypsy wedding, since he'd already been "married" to the mother of Miriam, but in the next-best version.

"Did you do the handkerchief?" I asked.

"No way," Diane says, with a shudder. "Twice, the marriage was called off because I refused. In the end, I slept with Moïse just to show him I was a virgin. We had the wedding in a restaurant. I had never tasted wine before: one glass, and I passed out. The next morning, I looked at this rose in a glass by my bed, I said, What's that for? My mother said, What's that for? It's for—*baffe*—she smacked me on the head."

"Your *mother*? You didn't spend your wedding night with Moïse?"

"Of course not. *Chez les Gitans,* you go home to your own house, and the next day, your husband comes for you."

In retrospect, it was a match of genius. Diane was high-strung, Moïse apparently calm. Diane was smart and literate (it's she who pays the bills and keeps Tekameli's clippings file in perfect order), Moïse was a potential earner. Both were tolerant. Moïse isn't a jealous husband, Diane is not a suspicious wife—on the contrary, she has a seemingly limitless willingness to believe his tall tales. By St. Jacques standards, they had money to burn. Theoretically, they should have had a ball together.

But there's this awful twist to life in St. Jacques. Your husband or wife is by definition the last person on earth with whom you can have a good time. Fun by definition is what happens the moment you leave your spouse behind. Your husband is the person who staggers through the door for a sleep and a change of clothes; your wife is the person who's scrubbing the floors, ironing your shirts, raising your children while you're gone. In the rare moments you see her, you are tired and hungover, she has a Vesuvian backload of frustration and demands, and St. Jacques etiquette teaches you that the wisest thing to do is smack her black-and-blue before she has a chance to open her mouth. Even Saint Moïse, according to Garth and Pascale, once landed Diane in the emergency ward. Why? "Because she hadn't done the dishes?" Pascale speculates.

Besides, Moïse loved children, and Diane didn't. She didn't feel ready to be a mother. "I didn't want the responsibility; I only wanted to party. I handed Kevin to my mother for the first two years of his life. Finally she said, If you don't take your son back, I'm getting custody"—i.e., it would be Antoinette who would receive child benefits from the French state. "I took him back, and I spoiled him so rotten he was a monster. At school, he used to pee all over the other children, at nap time, he'd walk up and down the aisle, poking his finger into their eyes. It's a miracle he's turned out such a kind, polite boy. After Kevin, Moïse had to beg me for nine years before I agreed to have another child."

And Moïse, who wanted a big brood, who—along with his mother-in-law—is the one who actually looks after Kevin and the baby, went elsewhere.

"In 1998, Guy Bertrand and I were taking Tekameli on tour to Australia," says Garth. "We were supposed to leave the fourth of January."

On December 31st, a sealed judgment arrived at Guy's house: Moïse was being summoned to appear before a Languedoc-Roussillon tribunal on January 5th, no fail.

"What was the matter?"

"There was this woman in Carcassonne who'd had four children by Moïse, and she thought it was time he paid up."

Trying to wangle him out of court on New Year's Eve was no joke, but they managed.

"What did Moïse say?"

"We never discussed it," replies Garth. "If Diane's bonkers, I'd say she had provocation. These women don't have much of a life. You know, José walks into the Casa, it's Saturday afternoon. I ask him, Where's your wife? At home. Why don't you bring her along? She's got housework. Well, the girl is sixteen at most. Why don't *you* try sweeping the house for once? You ever tried washing a dish, José? You should; it's a blast, you'd really enjoy it."

Diane's life, by Gypsy standards, is irreproachable: she is married to a scion of St. Jacques, she wears black to her ankles, never leaves the apartment without a proper escort. But whereas Linda can do no wrong, Diane is still regarded as a loose cannon, dangerously wacky.

The childhood typecasting—that Linda is the good girl, Diane the bad—survives.

4

Sunday evening. The bright daylight has faded, and Linda has moved the sleeping Marlon from her lap to his stroller. It's time to start thinking about going home, about what to make for dinner. Tomorrow is a school-day.

The sisters are still mulling over the story of Linda's long romance with Mario, over whether she should have gone to Paris to join her childhood sweetheart.

Diane has no doubts. "You missed your chance," she tells Linda. "You haven't experienced life, you haven't had any fun." To me, "She has never drunk, she's never smoked, she won't go to clubs. What kind of life's she had? It's only church, work, sleep."

Linda snorts. "I'm not missing anything but a lot of fools making fools of themselves! My idea of a good time is friends talking together like this, or going out to hear a good band, not doping yourself unconscious to earsplitting music."

"I am stronger than you," insists Diane. "I'm not afraid to live."

"You are strong in your *conneries*," Linda retorts.

"Suck up, teacher's pet, ass-kisser," taunts Diane. "Little Miss Priss who hates naughty girls, Daddy's little angel . . ."

"It's true," confesses Linda to me, laughing. "Whenever our father was angry and about to hit me, I'd straightaway start howling and he'd melt. Whereas Diane would provoke him. She'd say, real defiant, Go on, hit me, you coward! and get smacked twice as bad."

All of a sudden, it's Diane who's snuffling, sobbing, tears rolling down her cheeks. "I've fucked up my life, I've fucked up my life!" she wails.

Linda and I reassure her, "You have two wonderful children, a husband who loves you."

"I'm *not* strong; I get sick all the time."

But the next moment, because these Gypsies are volatile, Diane's up and dancing around the room. "I love my sister, I love my sister!" she sings.

"Get your teeth fixed!" shoots back Linda, who's got a pearly-perfect white smile.

"I love you!" repeats Diane, of the rotten yellow-brown rat's snaggle.

"Go to the dentist!"

"I can't—I'm too scared!" says Diane, now laughing and crying at the same time.

5

There is this curious symmetry in the Meziani family which the children like to joke about. Linda was good, Diane was bad. Between the two brothers, there was a similar divide: Samir was the "hooligan," while Daniel, the baby of the family, was "perfect."

"Everyone was always saying to Diane, Why can't you be like your big sister? Everyone was always saying to Samir, Why can't you be like your little brother?"

Today, although the four grown children are inseparable, the clichés have paid off. The "good" children advanced into the *paio* world, and the "bad" children went Gypsy.

Daniel's sisters are immensely proud of him. Daniel finished high school and graduated from the prestigious University of Montpellier, with a degree in cinematography and plastic arts. He is married to his college girlfriend, Christine, whom his family adores.

"How could Daniel marry a Gypsy?" Linda demands. "He needed someone who could go to a Japanese manga film with him, and talk about it afterwards. A Gypsy wife would care for nothing but soaps."

Today Daniel is a teacher at a chess academy on the Avenue Foch.

I've heard a lot about Samir, too. Samir has a reputation as a funhead, a party boy, a drinker. He plays a little music. If a Tekameli singer doesn't show up for a tour, he's been known to fill in.

The first time I meet Samir, at Marlon's first birthday party, he does indeed appear *"un vrai Gitan."* He's just returned from a two-day bender in Barcelona with Moïse and Jérôme and Jérôme's pianist son Jonathan, and all four men are so hungover that daylight's obviously like a knife blade in the eye. Golden-skinned, with a broken front tooth and a boxer's squashed-flat nose, Samir's wearing a purplish-black zoot suit, several pounds' worth of gold, and a pair of yellow-tinted octagonal granny glasses.

Like all the Meziani kids, he's got a raw sweetness and generosity: Samir is who you'd want to come to if you were in trouble.

Like Diane, Samir married a *"petite cousine."* His wife, Bimba, looks like a harpy, two feet tall and three feet wide, black-clad, with beady eyes and a shrill voice. But in fact she's okay. Bimba comes from a hard-line St. Jacques family: if Gypsies were Jews, Bimba's family would be Hasidim. I'm probably the first non-Gypsy she's ever met socially, and once she's seen me often enough to summon up the nerve to speak to me, she is eager to tell me stories of how Palm Sunday or All Saints' Day is celebrated *chez nous*—warm self-assured stories of someone to whom the traditions have come down full-bodied, unbroken.

Samir and Bimba live with her parents in the Caserne on Place Puig, where residents are fond of throwing garbage on the heads of parents picking up their children from the adjacent school. Their only child, seven-year-old Maëva, is a gorgeous imp with what Manhattanites might call "behavioral issues": she pinches babies, tortures small animals, spits at her teacher, doing all three in the space of about twenty seconds, and while laughing.

"Satan," says Diane, darkly.

In fact, Maëva's got the bad luck to be both intelligent and high-energy in a culture in which girls are best off brain-dead. Watching Maëva in her long black skirts leap, pirouette, somersault, I suggest to Diane and Linda that their niece might benefit from sports. Sports? That's for boys. The only exercise Maëva needs is a good spanking.

Samir lives the St. Jacques life, but according to Linda, he has regrets. "He's still retained the Parisian mind-set, but he has to hide it. Before his marriage, he was an after-school counsellor, which he loved, but when he married Bimba, he had to quit his job and find Gypsy work."

"Why?"

Linda looks ironical. "He couldn't exactly show up in the office in his Gypsy clothes! Besides, a Gypsy doesn't *work*. He cuts his little deals, but no way can there be some fixed hour at which he wakes up in the morning and has to *be* somewhere. Can you imagine a Gypsy with an alarm clock? Samir buys and sells in the markets across France." ("No guns, no drugs, no contraband," Samir tells me, laughing, "but everything just short.") He's sad, he misses his other life, sometimes he even talks about moving back to Paris, but he never will.

"Samir's given up so much," Linda goes on. "You know, you won't believe it, but in the old days, he loved to play chess!"

Meanwhile, I am getting the impression that being a St. Jacques Gypsy requires being dumb.

But, paradoxically, it is Samir, the naughtiest of the naughty Mezianis, who obliges the others to be extra-good. Samir, because of his wife Bimba, is the most deeply ensconced in the St. Jacques establishment. When Diane wants to smoke on the street or go hear an R & B band for her birthday, it's "think of your brother's reputation" that constrains her. When Linda begins to date a Frenchman, she sees him in secret, so Gypsies won't give Samir a hard time.

What results is a split between private license and a public face, where Moïse and Samir supposedly don't mind what their women do as long as they themselves aren't hassled about it: an instinctive doubleness familiar to anyone raised in a strict religion.

But what differentiates *"la loi gitane"* from Judaism or Islam or more fundamentalist brands of Christianity is that there is no corresponding code of male probity, nor is there any sense of divine will behind the prohibitions. Gypsy laws, it seems, are made not to glorify God but merely to spite women!

6

Linda manages—just barely—to exist in two worlds. "But it's not liveable," she admits.

"Why do you choose to stay in St. Jacques?"

Linda reflects. "It's your family," she says. "Within that family, there is enormous warmth, solidarity, support.

"If a Gypsy sees another Gypsy in trouble, he jumps in, no matter what. What would I do in Paris, a single mother with no money, no connections? Here I have my sister and brothers, my aunts, my cousins. Every day, I eat at my mother's house; my washing machine is broken, I take my laundry downstairs to Diane's."

This familialness, this cupboard-love is intrinsic to a larger Mediterranean culture, in which sons go into the family business and bring their wives to live in their parents' house, in which loyalty, duty, respect for elders, and the collective good take precedence over modern notions of self-fulfillment. Behind these customs lies the understanding that the world is a vicious place in which loners get devoured by wolves, that it's only by sticking together and looking after one's own that there's any hope of getting by.

One night at an open-air concert during the Casa Musicale's three-day music festival in St. Jacques, I get a peripheral glimpse of Gypsy solidarity. There are stars from Mali, Algeria, Brazil, Marseille, playing alongside local St. Jacques bands, and the Gypsies are out in full force, turning the Esplanade to a sea of black and gold and baby carriages. Diane goes off to buy us *merguez* sandwiches, pushing Marlon in his Mack truck of a stroller.

"Leave him with me," I suggest.

She hesitates, then looks around. Behind us, there's a gang of little Gypsy boys, the oldest barely up to my chest.

"Look after these two, will you?" Diane charges them.

"What's the matter, you don't trust me?"

"You don't know this neighborhood, Fernande."

For ten minutes, I enjoy the weird back-to-front of being "protected" by a bunch of eight-year-olds. Then I return to my own freedom.

There is indeed a Mafia effect to Gypsydom—within the crippling confines, you feel immensely safe, as women are said to feel when their battering husbands are in a tender mood.

7

Since her daughter Tanya was a little girl, Linda's been preparing her passage into the French mainstream. Tanya is more than ready to go. "She has no Gypsy friends," Linda tells me. "She's too old to talk to boys, and her girl cousins she has nothing in common with. Tanya's interested in literary theory. They are interested in husbands. She wants to talk about hip-hop. They want to talk about how many pearls they're going to have on their wedding dresses."

"Any chance she'd marry a Gypsy?"

"Never, never, never. Daniel couldn't, neither could I, she even less so. Tanya has no sympathy for my capacity to be at home in two worlds simultaneously. She is straighter."

While Tanya remains in Perpignan, she "obeys the rules."

"I explain to her, It's not that I don't trust you—it's because *they* are so vile they are only looking to spread slander."

"Does she feel more constricted than her school friends?"

"On the contrary, her friends are all *Maghrebines,* who have older brothers breathing down their necks, making sure they don't sully the family honor. They are the youngest of eight, ten children, so their mothers are old. Tanya feels lucky to have a mother so close to her age, with whom she can talk openly about teenage needs. And I am pretty free with her. I tell her, Wait till you get to Montpellier, you can have your own apartment, you can go on the Pill.

"But it must be said that women are forcing change on the Gypsy world. Already there are enough women who have their driver's licenses, who work. When they go to the beach, they want to swim, and they refuse to wade into the shallows in black skirts. You see groups of young girls downtown, whereas ten years ago they needed a grandmother as chaperone; you see engaged couples out alone together."

Linda leans back, arms crossed over her chest, and gazes into the distance. "You want to know my ideal? I want to be French and live as I choose, and *yet* be accepted by Gypsies.

"For me, that will never happen, it's still too soon." She sighs. "In truth, I don't know who will ever live to see that day."

Chapter Nine

1

Once only in our acquaintance does Moïse ask me a favor.

"You live out in the country?"

"Yeah."

"Do you know someone who could rent me a little parcel of land?"

I look puzzled.

"Not much—just three square meters. Enough to keep a rooster on. Here, in St. Jacques, they get stolen."

Unfortunately, it's one thing I can't do for him. Few locals will rent to Gypsies. It's an endless source of hassle.

A year later, his son Kevin raises the subject again. "About that plot of land for the fighting cock . . ."

This is Moïse's passion. He loves fighting cocks. He likes to raise and train the roosters himself, he likes to hang out with fighting-cock breeders, and discuss different breeds and techniques; he likes to go to the matches.

Kevin, too, is crazy about fighting cocks—it's one of the things he and his father do together. If Kevin had a rooster of his own, he tells me, he would never throw it into the junkheap if it lost a match. He would nurse it lovingly to old age, combing it, bathing it, feeding it choice tidbits. Hell, Kevin wouldn't even mind having a *hen*.

Cockfighting is a favorite St. Jacques sport. You can't cross the neighborhood without spotting a rooster in someone's garage, or even strutting about at liberty in the Place Puig. Male chitchat tends to revolve around favorite training methods—this one prefers bathing them in white-wine vinegar; the other swears lemon juice is the best antibiotic; before the fight, you feed them less so their legs get muscly from raking for grain.

Cockfights are illegal in France. But there is a loophole, which reveals a softer aspect to those French passions both for regulation and for "tradition": practices which are illegal in the rest of France are permitted in areas in which they are an attested part of a people's local heritage.

Thus, in the south of France, certain Latinisms such as bullfights and cockfights are allowed although, since cockfights also involve gambling, they are in theory allowed, but in practice absolutely pain-of-death secret. There are Gypsy cockfights in Roussillon almost every weekend, although you will never see an advertisement for one, or meet a Gypsy who will tell you where they take place, or a *paio* who has been to one.

2

One Saturday in May, Moïse takes me to a cockfight.

"Look after Fernande, Mo," Diane warns. "Don't let her out of your sight."

I may not think Gypsies are dangerous, but Diane does.

This is no ordinary cockfight. This is the Perpignan championship.

Kevin, who customarily appears almost superhumanly composed and genial, is beside himself. Moïse won't let him come to the fight, because Kevin is supposed to be training for his full-contact championship in two weeks. When his father swings past the vacant lot where he is playing soccer with his gang—his best friend, Banna, a gangly Senegalese boy, and two smaller Arab brothers—Kevin kicks Moïse's car and won't say goodbye. When he looks up, his cheeks are red and tear-streaked.

Instead, we drop by the rue des Carmes, and pick up from a house catercorner to the Jérôme-Jeanne-Francisquet-Antoinette strip a thirteen-year-old cousin of Moïse's called Samuel Cargol. Samuel Cargol is tall and fat—fat in a manner that in olden days would be prized, along with his rosy cheeks, thick glossy hair, and even white teeth, as token of a rude animal health. He is dressed in a pearl-gray-Adidas tracksuit that must have cost his mother a princely sum, and he exudes a good-humored self-confidence. Samuel Cargol is the grandson of Pitou Cargol. Samuel, at thirteen, already has an patrician air to him. You suspect you are meeting a future godfather of St. Jacques. Moïse explains to me through which ancestors both he and Diane are related to Samuel. It is the most complicated piece of brainwork I have ever heard him execute, but it makes them all, like everybody else in St. Jacques, *petits cousins.*

Samuel climbs into the car: he had expected, as a male, to sit up front, and is surprised when I retain that privilege. He and Moïse begin to chat in high-speed Gitan. They don't talk adult to child, but man to man, companionably. Samuel goes to every cockfight in Roussillon, and he is pleasantly knowledgeable on the subject.

We continue to weave through the backstreets of St. Jacques. You can hear Tekameli's "O Madre" blasting from an apartment window—you can always hear a Tekameli song from someone's window in St. Jacques—but Moïse doesn't appear to notice. It gives him no visible kick to hear his songs played, any more than it does to be told that posters of his album are plastered all over music stores in London or New York.

Moïse *always* drives through St. Jacques, no matter in what direction he's headed. Straightaway he cuts off the big boulevard on which he and Diane live—a ring road that provides shortcuts across Perpignan and to outlying villages and suburbs—and ensnarls himself in the snaky labyrinth of St. Jacques alleys. He cruises, slow-slow, through double-parked streets barely wide enough for one car. Pedestrians and other drivers look to see whom he's with; everybody checks out everybody. Four, five times a day—every time he gets in his Kyoto—Moïse drives through St. Jacques, the way you might turn on the radio to hear the news.

Although Moïse, like Diane, tells you that he hates Gypsies, that he has nothing to do with Gypsies, that he would be happy if he never laid eyes on another Gypsy as long as he lives, and that St. Jacques in particular he regards as the pits, although he claims that the greatest benefit of his musical success has been the chance to get out in the world and meet *paios*—uh, I mean, *Français*—in fact, the *only* thing in the world that interests him is other Gypsies.

I have seen Moïse cross a large crowded department store on the Spanish border in order to get a light from a man he has never seen before, but whom he spots as a fellow Gypsy. He leans toward the man, silent, cigarette in his mouth, and the man lights his Marlboro, also without a word, yet the current of tacit kinship between them, the quickening of interest, the relief at finding one of your own in such a smelly throng of *paios*, is palpable.

The cockfight is being held in a place I've had described to me, but in which I could never hope to set foot unless I was "brought," a place so infamously off-limits that you wonder if the postman dares deliver mail there. This place lies on the plain, in a patch of abandoned scrubland between the villages of Bompas and Pia, but as far as I know, it has no name. It is not autonomous enough to be considered a village—there isn't a single store—nor is it near enough to anything to be called a suburb. It has the organic logic of a refugee camp, a place government-built to solve a problem. In this case, it is the problem of a nomadic people who have now become more or less sedentary, but who have no intention of acclimatizing themselves to their "host" country.

It is a settlement not of Catalans but of Andalusians, Spanish-speaking Gypsies whose focal center is the south of Spain and who are much more mobile, much more wild, and reputedly much more violent and lawless than their St. Jacques cousins. Catalan Gypsies in Roussillon consume drugs, but it's Andalusian Gypsies who sell them. And these two tribes, supposedly, are at each other's throats.

We turn off a small rural road into the settlement. It's a public-housing development of single-story cement bunkers, but there's been some attempt to relieve the army-issue penury of the place: the houses are painted a tropical mango, and the streets laid out in curves and semi-circles. The walls are covered in the usual Gypsy child graffitti of Tatiana=J, and Sara=B. There are numerous trailers parked in the scrubland-turned-dump behind the houses, and still-smoldering fires from cookouts and garbage-burnings, alongside broken chairs and sofas with sprung stuffing. The families who own these houses don't necessarily live in them. They tend, like Jeannot's extended family, to have serial plots of land around Spain and France, spending a couple of months in each, and to sleep in their caravans.

There are no men on the streets, and the women and children are of a ragged and prematurely wizened toothlessness. The streets have no names, but Moïse knows exactly where we're going. We have arrived, as is his wont, painfully early—at 11:45, for a show scheduled for one—but there are already half a dozen cars parked.

A sudden flurry of agitated Gitan breaks out between Moïse and Samuel. Moïse, it turns out, has last-minute cold feet about bringing me. As we open the front gate of the house where the championship is taking place, Samuel coaches me on the story they've agreed upon. Whatever you do, don't say you're a journalist. If anybody asks, tell them you're a musician.

We come into the house through the garage, where a blonde Manush and two little girls are frying bacon and *merguez,* and putting them into baguettes. The price for a sandwich, which the woman quotes in old francs, abolished in the '60s, is wartime high. When I pay up, she pretends I am trying to palm foreign money off on her, and gives me back ludicrously too little change.

These are the last females I see, and the last piece of unfriendliness, for the event is as male as Mount Athos—no hens, no *paios*—and uniformly jolly.

Moïse and Samuel and I pay our fifty-franc entrance fee, and are let through a barricade.

3

The event is taking place in the backyard of the president of the Cockfighters' Association. With admirable economy, this short, powerfully-built Spaniard, with a walrus moustache and a white, gap-toothed grin, has transformed his small backyard into an all-weather arena. There is a corrugated plastic roof overhead, and two rows of bleachers on three sides—wooden planks placed on concrete blocks, which are resting on top of the roosters' double-stacked cages. (It is a strange sensation, to be sitting on top of a rooster—either it is trying to peck at your calves, or you are having to squeeze over, while its anxious owner reaches between your legs to water the bird, and clean it, and ready it for the fight.)

In the middle of the yard, on cement blocks covered in a strip of blue-green carpet, is the ring: a transparent plastic-sided circle, maybe two feet high.

The stadium fills slowly. By the time the match begins, there are a hundred men crammed into a tiny space. For a Gypsy gathering, there are remarkably few children, and not a girl among them.

The home crowd, and the majority of the spectators, are Andalusians, but there are also a couple of dozen Catalan Gypsies from St. Jacques, and a small group of blue-eyed blonds who turn out to be Manush. Three languages—Spanish, Catalan Gitan, and French—are being spoken simultaneously and interchangeably. The event thus represents something of a diplomatic congress, and the St. Jacobites are uncharacteristically civil and ingratiating.

It's the first time I've encountered Andalusian Gypsies in Roussillon, and they prove a different breed from the fat, unhealthy Catalans of St. Jacques. These are proud, handsome men, with dark-brown skin, flashing eyes, and lithe strong bodies. If you can imagine "machismo" being reclaimed from a term of disapprobation, these men, with their easy grace and high spirits, might do it.

They speak a jovial and highly declamatory Spanish. Whenever a popular fellow shows up, there are loud cheers and shouts of *Olé!* and *Arriba!* and everyone appears to be called either Titou or Tatou, or Chatou or Chabou or Chinou. They are wearing fantastical quantities of gold, even by Gypsy standards, including as many as four hefty rings on each hand, and, unlike the Catalans, they are heavily tattooed.

Much of the ornamentation is religious, but even more is familial. One young hunk wears a baby's pacifier on his key chain, while other men's biceps are emblazoned in the names of family members—"My heart belongs to Mina. Ramon. Luisa. José." or "My wife is a rose."

There is an abundance, too, of involuntary tattooing: most cheeks and arms, and—as becomes evident as the men strip in the afternoon heat—chests and stomachs bear formidable weals of purple-pink scar tissue.

The championship doesn't actually start till two. The preceding hours are taken up by the inspection and weighing of the roosters, the matching of who is to fight whom, and the placing of bets, all of which occurs in the president's chandeliered living room, behind the privacy of white lace curtains.

The cocks have come from Belgium and Spain and the Balearic Islands and as far away as Guadeloupe. Some are brindle golden, some petrol green with iridescent tail feathers, some have bleached-blond plumage overlying the black, which creates the same sinister beauty as in their Gypsy owners who peroxide streaks and quiffs of their black hair. The roosters' underbodies have been shaved, which gives them the appearance of giant pink strawberries. A few have artificial spurs sewn onto their heels for extra bite.

The owners stroke their birds, spray them from atomizers to cool them down, wipe their smeared assholes clean with white cloths, murmur to them encouragingly. The roosters have names like Ace or Demon, suggesting rage, speed, menace. The Andalusians refer to their hopped-up highbreeds laughingly as *"pollos,"* but "chicken" does little to convey the high-strung grace and compact menace in these beasts.

It is a boiling hot day, after a cold gray spring. In the afternoon sun, the plastic-roofed arena becomes an oven. It is not just hot, but dangerously hot, the hottest place I've ever been. I feel like a clandestine being sneaked across the border in a sealed truck, and wonder if I will get cooked alive.

I am sitting at the end of a plank in the front row, so shoved over I can only fit half a buttock on the bleacher, while the men sprawl their legs wide. When the cramp gets too bad, I stand up. Every now and then, an Andalusian will come over and tell me to get the other men to give me some room, and since I don't dare, he himself will tell all the guys to shove over. Heaving aggrieved sighs, the men make a few inches' space, and for five minutes maybe I've got my whole bottom on the plank, but although they are friendly enough, it obviously doesn't seem quite right to them that I should have room to sit down, so pretty soon I get shoved off again. Being a woman in Gypsy land, I gather, is like being the runt of the litter.

The atmosphere is loud and jolly. Everybody is having lots and lots of fun, and the heat—although calamitous for the roosters—is the source of much romping. The Andalusians spray themselves and each other with their atomizers, affectionately dousing their neighbors' heads, necks, underarms. "Chanel!" laughs one. (I've noticed that Gypsies don't smell of sweat as other southern French do. In these suffocatingly close quarters, the only scent is of aftershave.) Moïse gets sprayed by a friend, and I am handed an atomizer to spray myself.

As it gets more and more sweltering under the corrugated plastic in the afternoon sun, everybody strips, and one dark handsome man in a rust-red corduroy shirt draws a switchblade from his trousers and, without removing his shirt, slices off the sleeves at the shoulder, and rips great vents up the seams as far as his armpits.

4

At last, the fights begin.

There are twenty-five matches, that is, fifty roosters fighting today, half of whom are going to end up dead. Each owner has the choice of giving his fighter fake spurs, but Titou is one of the few who chooses to do so.

Titou, the owner of Furian, is in his late thirties. Wiry, bald, with a raunchy grin, his body blue with tattoos, he moves as if on a tight-coiled spring, like Popeye on crank.

Standing in the ring, Titou opens a tin Navy Cut box containing syringes, needle, thread, spurs, tape. He puts the spur—which resembles an artificial fingernail—on his rooster, wraps it in tape, bites off the spare tape with his teeth, and chews it to a pulp which he eventually spits out like a wad of tobacco. He sews on the spur, then shoots up his rooster with amphetamines, which makes the bird tremble uncontrollably.

When the fight begins, Titou on the sidelines humps his groin, roaring with laughter, shouting at Furian to fuck his opponent. The spectators all laugh, but Furian still gets creamed.

5

The initial encounter inevitably has a nervous jolt of beauty. When they are first placed in the ring, the two roosters are shocked by the sight of the other. Necks extended, beak to beak, they stare each other down like an animal eyeballing itself in the mirror. One will peck, while the other circles his adversary in a jerky tribal war dance of intimidation.

Then they jump over each other's heads, again and again, with a whirring of wings, in tall ninja leaps. They leap to get away from the other's pursuing beak; they leap in order to deliver a spurred kick. That is the most beautiful part of the fight.

A fight lasts anywhere from eight to a dull, agonizing twenty minutes. (There's a clock.) What's wretched about cockfighting, I discover, is that there are few even matches. Some of these roosters are pros who know exactly what to do—that is, rip open the enemy's jugular—some are even the victors of three or four previous fights, but most of them don't seem to have a clue what to aim for.

Almost from the first instant's encounter, one rooster is visibly stronger and more aggressive, the other an increasingly passive defendant, seeking only to deflect the enemy's onslaught. I have been told that animals in the wild never fight to the death. One will always flee. In the ring, too, the weaker bird usually tries to run away, but is trapped by glass walls.

Peck-slash-whirr-leap-peck. Beak searches for throat, for eyes, spurs lash at underbelly. As they bite-kick-bite, the roosters' heads get increasingly bloodied, the blood spurts, spatters against the glass walls of the ring, and the front-row spectators—that means me and Samuel and Moïse—find their shirts and faces sprayed in gleaming viscous speckles of blood.

The rooster is half-blind—one eyeball has been pecked sightless—and he's increasingly disoriented. He dips, he staggers, he spins around wildly, trying to fight off an opponent he can no longer see. The enemy lands another nip on his neck, he's lost too much blood now, his one good eye is blinded by blood, he falls to the ground. And the soon-to-be victor, who himself has taken quite a beating, circles his fallen enemy in some confusion, not quite sure where to land the fatal blow. He wanders south to bite the bird on the leg, then mounts him for a final go at the jugular.

And this is the horrid part: the loser will not let himself die. Even when it's apparent from the first peck that his opponent is far stronger and more ruthless, it still takes a small eternity for the aggressor to have mangled his prey into a sufficiently inert state of horizontality for the match to be declared over. Just when he appears at last to be out cold, the rooster will pop back upright for a final stand, mutilated, eyeless, panting, weeping, and the fracas drags on for another two, three rounds.

Our survival instincts are just about unconquerable and

yet not always useful. Pretty soon all I am wishing is that the weaker rooster will just lie down and die fast, since there is no way out; he's going to end up on the garbage-heap no matter how brave he's been.

6

I am sitting next to one of the Manush, a small, neat, sociable redhead named Jacquot, who has three cocks in the match that he's bred and raised himself.

Jacquot tells me he comes from Carcassonne, a city seventy miles northwest of Perpignan. He and his family live there all winter, but come spring, they hitch up their trailers and travel around the country in a convoy of maybe forty trailers. Jacquot has been brought to this event by his nephew— a sun-bleached blond who looks like a surfer, with two sons between his knees—who lives in one of the villages outlying Perpignan.

Jacquot is keeping score, laboriously, in florid nineteenth-century-style numerals. (His writing evidently makes people nervous. Unlike me, he gets asked why he's there, and who brought him.)

The prizes go to the winners of the quickest matches— it's six thousand *ancien solde* for First Prize, five thousand for Second, and so on. But many of these matches are declared, as Jacquot mispells, *"nule,"* because the loser isn't properly dead.

Jacquot's first cock is one such loser. He is handed the bird, whom he lays between our feet. Jacquot bitterly watches his former favorite pant, sob, shudder, and bleed to death in a mess of broken glass and cigarette ash.

"Watch out," nudges a young Andalusian in chinos and bandanna, who has noticed that the rooster's death throes are freaking out a still-penned-up comrade, who, seeing what lies in store, is trying desperately to escape from its cage.

The Andalusian discreetly removes Jacquot's bird and throws it in the garbage. "All my birds are going to lose," Jacquot complains. "I shot them up with antibiotics just before the match, and it's made them weak."

7

After the twelfth match—the best, because the cocks were well-paired, and both wanted to fight—Moïse and Samuel and I agree that it's too hot, and cut out. Moïse thinks it's been a good day, and says the championship will probably go on till one in the morning—which means a total of twelve hours.

He asks me if I enjoyed it, and I, sifting through the layers of interest, boredom, exquisite discomfort, squeamishness, and self-disgust I'd felt at this spectacle, which seemed closer to a flea circus than a bullfight, lie and say yes. Moïse asks me if I would come back, and this time I say maybe, but I know he can tell I wouldn't. There's no way either of us can know that later on, like many of the boring times I spend with the Gypsies, it will seem like one of the best days of my life.

This time—on the ride back to St. Jacques, past artichoke fields and villages still with their defensive walls of red-brick-and-rough-stone *cayrou*—Samuel sits up front.

I hear Samuel ask Moïse why I'd come, and Moïse answer, "She's *curiosa*. Besides, she's a journalist."

"What's that?"

"A journalist is someone who likes to see things—all kinds of things—to find out what they're like."

I can imagine more high-minded or more hostile definitions of a journalist, but to me, Moïse's definition pretty much covers the basic impulse.

Samuel asks me where I'm from.

"New York."

Samuel doesn't know where New York is—this is six months before September 11th, when everyone in the world, even St. Jacques Gypsies, finds out about New York.

"It's in America."

"Is America in California?"

"Other way round."

"Do you know Van Damme?"

"Who?"

He raises his fists to illustrate.

"No, but I met Arnold Schwarzenegger before he was a movie star, back when he was just a bodybuilder."

"Who's he?" asks Samuel.

"A star from before your time."

Chapter Ten

1

This wasn't the first time Samuel and I had met, although I was surprised he recognized me in such a different setting.

Two months earlier, there had been a conference at Collège Jean Moulin, the Gypsy junior high school in St. Jacques which Moïse and the Mezianis all attended, however briefly. The conference was about Gypsy education, and it was intended for *"pédagogues."* The evening before, I dropped by to see if I could sit in on it.

Collège Jean Moulin is an enormous nineteenth-century Spanish-style barracks, catercorner to the Casa Musicale. The receptionist deposits me in the principal's waiting room, which is empty except for a rosy-cheeked fat boy in a three-piece khaki nylon jogging suit, whom I automatically assume is being hauled before the principal for some infraction.

The boy and I are shown together into the office. The principal's name is Paul Landric. He's a barrel-chested, crew-cutted Catalan, who looks more like a police chief or a foot-ball coach than a "pedagogue"—an appearance quite handy for someone running what's called in current French jargon a ZEP school *(Zone d'Education Prioritaire)*. Awaiting us is the boy's homeroom teacher, and a crew from Radio Roussillon.

Samuel Cargol isn't in trouble, he's the star. Radio Roussillon is covering the next day's conference, and Samuel has been chosen to represent both the perils and the potentials of Gypsy education.

The radio reporter, a young blond man, begins by interviewing Paul Landric. Sometimes I insert my own questions, sometimes Samuel's teacher offers an opinion. The occasion is pretty merry. People who work with Gypsies tend to laugh a lot. It's a laughter of hysterical exasperation, because if you didn't laugh, you'd hang yourself or quit. Get together two *paios* in the Gypsy social-welfare business, and all they do is one-up each other with tales of their charges' outrageousness.

Here's what we are told. There are 185 students in Jean Moulin, 150 of whom are Gypsies. (The remaining thirty-five belong to a special program of advanced music students from the conservatory, who are kept in quarantine from the rest of the student body.)

An average French junior high school freshman is twelve years old. The majority of Jean Moulin's first-year students, who tend to be a bit older, have never been to school before. About eighty percent of them, Paul Landric figures, can neither read nor write. They are already too far behind to catch up with the school curriculum, so most drop out.

"Gypsy students aren't dumb," Landric says. "They have the intellectual capacity to do well, especially the girls, but they lack the desire and the habits. They have no experience of organizing their time. The challenge is to convince students—and their parents—that they *need* school."

The conventional wisdom that an education will earn you a good living is no longer valid in high-unemployment France, he continues. How on earth can you convince these children that they should pursue knowledge for its own sake, acquire an education for the gentlemanly pleasure of possessing a well-stocked mind?

I ask the principal how Gypsy students compare to Arabs—a loaded question, since the children of North African immigrants are generally portrayed as being France's most explosive social problem.

"Oh, it's a different universe," Paul Landric promptly replies. "Maghrebian students are pushed enormously by their parents who, even if they are illiterate or, worse still, unemployed, hugely value education and hard work. They can see elders in the community who are professionals, who own their own businesses. The Gypsies, by contrast, have *zero* role models. There are no adults in their world who work. In all the years I've taught at Jean Moulin, there is only one Gypsy who has gone on to *lycée* [continued school past eighth grade], and him, his family moved him to another part of town so their friends and neighbors wouldn't haze him."

(When I repeat this anecdote to Linda, she knows exactly which boy he's thinking of. Oh sure, Jean Ramonet— the Ramonets were always different. He went on to study business, so he could take over his parents' store.)

"If an Arab kid cuts school, he stays in the street so his parents don't find out. If a Gypsy plays hookey, it's *in order* to stay home. Here, it's the parents who are the disruptive influence, mothers who want to coddle their sons, fathers who don't want their daughters to be seen hanging with boys at school. The girl is a commodity, and they don't want her to lose her market value."

"Although these youngsters are bored stiff hanging out at home, watching TV, they don't know they're bored, and the habits of discipline are too difficult to acquire."

Samuel has been sitting still throughout this discourse. Now it is his turn. The young journalist strikes a tone of jokey camaraderie with Samuel, the tone in which someone just beyond boyhood talks to someone who is still a boy—a tone quite different from Moïse's respectful man-to-man.

"What's your name?"

"Samuel Cargol."

Cargol is one of the dominant clans of Perpignan. When you hear the boy's name, it identifies him as part of the ruling élite. You know that unless Samuel's immediate family has sinned, he will grow up, if he chooses, to be one of the pastors who have access to municipal sinecures, government perks.

The journalist, although he lives in Perpignan, has never heard the name "Cargol." He is used to interviewing rugby players, the head of the Chamber of Commerce, visting celebrities. He has probably never spoken to a Gypsy before.

I ask Samuel if he's related to Pastor Pitou Cargol.

"He's my granddaddy."

Samuel is a baby-faced prepubescent thirteen. He isn't articulate—there are lots of questions that stump him—but he's frank and agreeable, in a rough, husky, Gypsy-Catalanized French, in which every word has a long trailing tail of *a*'s.

Samuel has just started sixth grade. It's not his first bout of schooling—he tried it once or twice before, but dropped out.

"Why did you start now?"

"All my friends were in school, I got bored staying home."

"How many years will you stay at school?"

Two more years, he thinks. Till he's fifteen.

Why no further?

He has no background. His father can't read or write, his older sister has never been to school. If his friends stay on, he might too, but he doubts it.

"Can you read now?"

Samuel wriggles. "A little," he says, doubtfully.

"What do you read?"

"Things," he says, reluctantly.

"What kind of things?"

He doesn't know.

"Comic books?"

"Yes," he says, relieved to have an answer supplied for him.

"What are your favorite pastimes?"

He doesn't know. Once again, the journalist guides him into answers: music, soccer, computer games. (Cockfighting isn't offered as a possible hobby.)

"What do you do after school?"

He has dinner at home, and after dinner, he goes out with his friends. They play soccer in Place Puig until the streetlights are turned off, then they go downtown, they buy snacks and play computer games till the bars close, then they wander the streets. They go to bed around one, two a.m. In the morning, he's too tired to get up.

"Too hard. *Fatigué, fatigué.*"

"Do you go to school every day?"

No. He almost always goes on Tuesdays and Fridays, especially the afternoons, but the other days it's too tiring. Usually he sleeps till around one.

"What's good about school?"

"You learn to count."

"Who are your friends?"

"Gitans."

"Do you know any French children?"

"No."

"Do you speak to them at school?"

"No."

"Have you ever played with a French kid?"

"No."

"Not even a game of soccer in the street?"

"No." He reflects and adds, "I see them sometimes, but I've never spoken to one."

The French flag flutters outside the principal's window, the Declaration of the Rights of Man is framed on the wall. I wonder if it strikes the other adults in the room as unsettling that Samuel Cargol, whose family has been in France for generations, refers to strangers as "French," and has never spoken to one, aside from schoolteachers.

The interviewer now questions Samuel's teacher.

"The boy's progressing," says his teacher. "He's beginning to accept that school life is different from street life, for example, no smoking in the classroom, but he's going to have to make a real effort if he's ever going to learn to read and write."

"Is he a difficult kid?"

"Are you difficult, Samuel?"

Samuel, laughing, admits, "I'm a big complainer."

"When are you going to marry?"

"I'll marry at eighteen, won't I?" he replies. "Maybe seventeen."

"Has your bride been chosen?"

"Not yet." (In fact, Samuel is married off at sixteen to the daughter of Mingo, a musician who lives in the Caserne.)

The interviewer asks Samuel whether he gets good grades. Samuel has never heard of grades.

"You know, the marks on the report cards your school sends home?"

He still looks blank.

Samuel's teacher, with a dry smile, enlightens the interviewer. Report cards belong to "the realm of paper." You know, an envelope arrives in the mail, probably the parents know it comes from the school, they recognize the school insignia, as opposed to welfare or a parking ticket, but it's *paper.* Maybe it's paper telling you about a school raffle or not to smoke in the corridors; they don't pay attention. "It's the realm of paper."

Paul Landric concludes, a touch wistfully, "Gypsy adolescence is too short. If only they gave us an extra three, four years, we could really make something of these kids. But at seventeen, they marry, at fifteen, they're already betrothed, and a betrothed person doesn't go to school."

2

The next day, Garth and I go to the conference.

The conference is entitled "The *scolarization* of children in the Gypsy community." French is a pompous language, but its usages often reflect reality: *scolarization,* as I've discovered from my own children, bears little relation to American notions of merely "going to school."

From the moment French preschoolers get their first vaccinations, they are being shaped into citizens of the Republic, which believes that there is one right way to do things, whether it's form the loop on your *f*'s or fry a potato or cure a cold or view the great ideological debates of our day.

But what I discover today is that when it comes to Gypsies, all this overbearing paternalism falters to a nervous halt. You've heard of "the French exception," France's version of American exceptionalism? Well, within the French exception, there is a Gypsy exception.

3

The conference opens with a panel discussion, then breaks up into workshops.

My group includes a school psychologist named Jean Casanova, who is also a local politician in the Green party; a French Caribbean nurse/nutritionist from Jean Moulin; my friend Garth Beattie from the Casa Musicale; Daniel Elzière, who has spent the last ten years teaching Manush children out of a campsite caravan; and Damienne Bourquin, a porky blonde who has just replaced her husband (who is now *conseiller général* of Languedoc-Rousillon) as the mayor of Millas, a nearby village with a large Gypsy population.

The rest of the workshop consists of teachers from Gypsy schools in Roussillon ranging from nursery school to high school. Participants take turns describing their own experiences, and offering prescriptions. There is a variety of outlooks expressed—from old-fashioned Republican authoritarian to liberal-multicultural to just plain romantic—Garth, for instance, suggests that the schools teach traditional Gypsy trades, such as shoeing horses and repairing carts. But most of the teachers who've come to this conference simply want a chance to feel not quite so alone in what's generally acknowledged to be a disheartening struggle.

Absenteeism is the opening topic. The reason Gypsy children don't go to school, most participants believe, is because they can't wake up in time. "Even the nursery-schoolers sleep all morning, because they've been up watching TV all night."

A bleeding-heart liberal suggests that they bring the mountain to Mahomet: "Why not adjust school to Gypsy hours?"

A primary-school headmistress shoots back, "At my school, we tried having late afternoon and night classes, and the children still didn't show up."

Now Jean Casanova, the school psychologist, launches in. "It's bullshit to maintain that sleeping all day is an inviolable part of the Gypsy cultural imperative. The Gypsies of Roussillon are a rural people who've historically lived by seasonal farmwork. Have you ever met farmworkers who can't get up in the morning to pick the crops?"

As one teacher points out, "Fifty years ago, the explanation for Gypsy illiteracy was nomadism: how could you go to school when you never spent more than a month in the same town? Now that government policies all over Europe have made sure the Gypsies are sedentary, they find Gypsies still don't want to go to school, and there's a whole new set of explanations."

Mme Bourquin, too, takes a tougher line. In her town of Millas, they've almost entirely solved the problem of absenteeism by cutting off welfare benefits to the families of truants. (A welfare official, on being told by Mme Bourquin of her Millas method, is appalled that anyone might be so barbaric as to use welfare payments in "an arsenal of punishment and repression.")

What Millas teachers have found, however, she continues, is that the real problem is what you actually do with these children once the dogcatcher has dragged them into the classroom. In her experience, there is a double whammy by which a younger generation of Gypsies have forgotten their own traditions, without acquiring the mainstream culture. "There's a terrible thinness to what they know. The grandparents are a hundred times more educated than their grandchildren; they left primary school literate and numerate."

A moony-looking woman wearing a peasant dress and long braids now raises her hand. "What I want to know is, why there are no Gypsies in our workshop? Why have they been excluded from our discourse? How can we talk about *them* without *them*?" (It's true: there are more Vietnamese people at the conference than Gypsies —the sole representative being a short cheerful pastor named Boy who works in the mayor's office.) "Isn't our talk of 'integration' a form of cultural genocide?"

Everybody in the workshop is audibly exasperated by this proposition, because, thank God, French people in general, and especially French pedagogues, really do still have an almost invincible sense of their own cultural and methodological superiority, and it's not so easy to persuade them that teaching a child to read and write is genocide.

"*What* culture?" says Garth. "The Gypsies of St. Jacques have no culture, and they know nothing about whatever culture they once had. All they have is their fear and their ignorance."

Jean Casanova, the school psychologist, now takes over. "The Gypsies of St. Jacques have managed to keep somewhat intact a seventeenth-century agrarian culture designed for seasonal pickers, small artisans, blacksmiths, market sellers, but its codes are in fact *hallucinants* (mind-blowing). This is Taliban-style fundamentalism. It's not just that Gypsies don't go to school long enough to learn how to read. What we are facing is a positive interdiction against literacy. Unless they cut themselves off from written language, they will be lost, they will disappear. Why should the Republic in any way encourage a culture based on barbaric taboos and on the absolute oppression of women? Our schools teach equality and access to power for everyone, which to Gypsy men is anathema. It's a culture of machismo in which the only way men can keep their power is by denying their sisters, wives, and daughters access to education, or any possibility of integration. It's a stranglehold—the fathers are preventing their children from learning because 'In their ignorance, we can keep our power.' We can't change their 'hours' effectively if we don't recognize this absolute conflict of values."

Garth remarks in his excellent French delivered with an ostentatiously Irish accent, "Everybody is talking about culture, but what about the law? There are French laws. Gypsies are French, but *the law does not apply to them*. There is a large, highly visible police station planted right in the middle of St. Jacques, but Gypsies break the law all day every day, while the police watch. There are places where the police won't go. There is a conspiracy of blindness which encourages them to misbehave."

This gives rise to a litany of familiar sarcasms, a round of sniggers about forged certificates of invalidism, of month-long medical exemptions from school that are rubbed ragged from having their dates erased and rewritten time after time.

"How come they're ninety percent illiterate, yet they manage very efficiently to work their way through a serpentine maze of welfare bureaucracy that would defeat most Ph.D. students and get their forms filled in and mailed by the due date?"

"If you just talk of law, you are talking of repression," objects one last bleeding heart.

"Not really," replies Maryse Martinez, an administrator from Jean Moulin. "Who is repressing whom? Let's not be romantic. If we give in to Gypsy fundamentalism, we are assisting in barbarity, we are assisting in a people's self-destruction through AIDS and inbreeding. And it's the women who pay, it's the daughters whose fathers lift them out of school in order to make them child brides. I hear Gypsy mothers who say, 'I don't want my daughter going to high school, because she will "escape."' This population *must* be liberated, it *must* evolve."

As in most discussions of Gypsies, the workshop concludes with the suggestion that the French state's best bet is the girls, "who have everything to gain and nothing to lose."

Most acknowledge, however, that the women's choices are painful. "There are two forms of integration," says Casanova. "They can marry non-Gypsies and get excommunicated, which is very hard. Or maybe they can find a middle strategy, one that's slyer. The girl can say, 'No, I won't get married at fifteen, maybe I'll wait till I'm twenty. Maybe I'd like to go to work, first. And maybe, once I'm married, I might prefer to have two children rather than six.' But this is hard, almost harder than outright defection. The revolt of women which has already happened among French Arabs creates painful family conflicts, and the men are often violent."

4

The conference embodied to me everything that was good and bad about Republican France. On the one hand, there was a staggering assumption of superiority. If these pedagogues were nineteenth-century missionaries to a cannibal island, they could not be more convinced that the belief system they wished to impose upon the Gypsy savages—in this case, egalitarian secularism—was as unequivocal a good as clean water.

But you also got the impression that within this bureaucracy, men and women were using their utmost powers of imagination and sympathy to devise ways of freeing a community that was clearly stuck and unhappy. Most of the people I met were struggling to find Gypsy solutions to Gypsy problems—the headmistress who said she had instituted evening classes for second- and third-graders who slept all day; or Daniel Elzière, who teaches Manush in their own caravans; or the nutritionist from Jean Moulin who told me that she'd taken part in a study commissioned by the mayor researching traditional Catalan Gypsy cooking, in order to see whether there were more wholesome great-grandmother's dishes that could be substituted for the diet of Doritos and Coca-Cola that was making young Gypsies so grotesquely overweight.

And this was the continuing oddity of my experience of official French approaches to Gypsies in Roussillon. Here, the age-old story of popular and official persecution which is being played out across the rest of Europe simply doesn't apply. True, people may give Gypsies dirty looks in the street, but they don't burn their houses down or shove shit through their mailboxes, as they do in Romania or Slovakia or even Germany and parts of northern France, and there are a number of laws, including one obliging communes to provide "travelers" with well-kept campgrounds and clean drinking water, that suggest officials are alert to any possibility of maltreatment.

After the conference, I ask Paul Landric how he thinks it went. On the whole, he's pleased, but the big questions remain.

How does he view the alternative to integration that was proposed—the notion of teaching Gypsies how to be Gypsy, much as ornithologists today teach bred-in-captivity cranes how to migrate?

It's sentimentality, he says. "People go on about Gypsies and music, but it's a dangerous fantasy. It's like basketball in a U.S. ghetto. How many kids actually end up being Michael Jordan? These kids pick up a guitar and they think they're Tomatito; *our* music students" [he is speaking of the thirty-five "French" students at Jean Moulin who are enrolled in the separate music program] "practice five hours every day of their lives."

To Paul Landric, the ideal remains "Gypsy modernity"— that is, the old-fashioned model of integration: Gitan at home, French in the streets. You come home from your job as a computer programmer, a travel agent, a salesman, and *then* you get out your guitar.

"People talk about preserving Gypsy culture. But what am I as an educator supposed to do when the comportment of my students is frankly pathological?"

5

It is common for humans to be bilingual, even trilingual, with at least one of those languages purely oral. When I go to friends' houses in Roussillon, I notice there is often a second language, a family language, that is spoken.

The phone rings, it's Caroline's mother, and suddenly she breaks into Gallego (the Galician dialect of Spanish). It's her brother, and now she's tripping back and forth in some private sibling intersplice of French, Spanish, Gallego. And she counts in Spanish.

My daughter, who has done all her schooling in France, counts in English. If she ends up an old woman in Cairo or Paris or Berlin, will she still count in English? The big cities of the West are places in which a thousand languages are dreamed in, counted in, cursed in.

Your mother tongue is often purely oral—either because it's a demotic dialect, such as Gallego or Gitan—or because your parents are illiterate in their native language. Most of my Maghrebian friends speak Arabic to their parents and siblings, but can't read or write it. A daughter of Algerian immigrants confesses that she studied the Koran in French, just to be able to outsmart her father, who, though illiterate, sealed every argument with "In the Koran it is written . . ."

Gitan is not a written language.

None of Roussillon's indigenous languages had an alphabet (the ratio of languages to alphabets in the world is probably about ten thousand to one: often the fit of sound to letter is procrustean, such as when the Turkic languages have been shoehorned variously into Arabic, Chinese, and Cyrillic alphabets).

The two reigning races in Roussillon in the Year One were Iberians and Celts, who intermarried easily, creating tribes and towns historians refer to, like some discount airline, as "Celtiberian." Iberian is a non-Indo-European language whose surviving inscriptions in Roussillon, transliterated into the Greek or Phoenician alphabets, and written indiscriminately from left to right and right to left, have been deciphered but not fully understood: that is to say, we can pronounce Iberian, but we don't know what we're saying. (I have a private theory, based on utter ignorance, that it might prove a granddaddy to Basque.)

The Celts, despite their bardic tradition, had no written language. Although the sons of the Celtic aristocracy were sent off to be schooled by druids, they did not learn to read or write: priestly teachings depended on secrecy, which meant that its élite had little interest in written transmission.

When the Romans conquered Gaul, they made a point of sending young aristocratic Celts to Rome for their education. The administration of empire is made easier by a written language. Gravestones show that late into the Roman Empire, prominent southern Gauls still bore distinctively Celtic names, just as assimilated French Arabs still call their children Rashida and Mourad. (To the extent that this habit is changing, it's so children won't be any further "stigmatized" at school or in the job market.) Oral languages are good for partisan fighting, for stubborn enclaves of resistance, for befuddling the colonizers. (In some places, such as Kurdish Turkey until a couple of years ago, speaking your "home" language can land you in jail.)

Can you teach me to speak Romany, Isabel Fonseca asks an acquaintance in *Bury Me Standing*, her account of modern-day Eastern European Gypsies. No, because as soon as we taught you a word, we'd have to find a new one, explains the friend. The name of God, too, is hidden. For language is intended not just to communicate, but also to conceal.

6

Where we live, French is the language of officialdom, of the desired mainstream, of integration, achievement, success.

Your mother tongue, whether immigrant or indigenous, is for being cozy by the fire, for sharing something private and delectable with your childhood playmates, for letting down your hair. (For Muslims, it's the language you revert to as soon as you've scuffed off your shoes.) In our village, the lean brown weather-beaten old ladies in aprons and felt slippers chatter in Catalan on a bench in the afternoon sun. The butcher teases his clientele in Catalan, and everybody dissolves into giggles, flicking an apologetic grin at the foreigner. "Even though I speak it badly, there are some things I can only say in Catalan," Dr. Morcrette tells me.

Not all home languages are equal. Adults are amazed to overhear my apparently French children chattering to me in English, as if it's some show-off parlor trick they're playing. My son's headmistress compliments me on the incalculable advantages of his bilingualism. She doesn't praise his classmate Djallal for his fluency in Arabic, or Johnny for speaking Gitan within his family circle. My children are not expected to "integrate."

Yet even though English is both the universal and the high-prestige language of today, I nonetheless derive a sneaky pleasure, the immigrant's revenge, in using fastball English to my family in front of friends and neighbors—the slurred, abbreviated, elliptical, and largely implicit shorthand of native speech.

Those votive medals inscribed in a jumble of Celtic, Iberian, and Latin that were found at the thermal springs in upcountry Roussillon and then lost reflect an ongoing human aptitude, latent, acquired, involuntary, for riding simultaneous cultures: French in the streets, Arabic at home; French at the office, Catalan in the kitchen.

But this division also marks the beginning of an ineluctable falling away into monoculture. Frédéric, who introduced me to Moïse, was raised by his Spanish Catalan grandparents, and knew no French when he started school. Today, when Frédéric's grandfather speaks to him in Catalan, Frédéric answers in French. Frédéric's wife, Hajiba, didn't learn French till her family immigrated from Morocco when she was eight. Hajiba and Frédéric's daughters understand neither Arabic nor Catalan.

These acquisitions and losses are a Mediterranean constant, accompanying the rise and fall of colonizing powers. You forget Berber, you learn Punic; you forget Punic, you learn Latin. Tato Garcia's grandfather is the last person in Roussillon to speak Kalo, the Spanish dialect of Romany: "He could not divulge it, even if he wanted to."

Often I wonder which paths the next generation of Mezianis will choose. Is Gypsy modernity a sustainable equilibrium, or merely a step to cultural extinction? For how many of them will St. Jacques mores, in which eight-year-old boys are allowed to drive cars, but their mothers aren't, seem impossibly remote? How many of Antoinette's great-grandchildren will be able to understand that disenvoweled shotgun variety of Catalan its speakers call Gitan?

To such *métisses*—children whose family languages also include Creole, Berber, Turkish, and Kurdish—French might seem like a massive relief, a welcome simplification—escape into enlightenment, efficiency, the job market.

Chapter Eleven

1

On a Thursday evening in April, I take my children over to Diane's house. We are preparing for an adventure: Palm Sunday, which for both Catalans and Catalan Gypsies is an even bigger deal than Easter. On Palm Sunday, the Gypsies have a feast. Diane and Linda's family variant is to drive up to the mountain border town of Le Perthus and have a big meal at a Spanish restaurant. After the feast, the children get photographed in their Palm Sunday best, carrying their palm branches.

The Palm Sunday photographs are the centerpiece of the day. Gypsy mothers spend months planning their children's outfits and devote much ingenuity to constructing the palm branches the children carry, from which cascades of candies are suspended. I have seen Diane's and Linda's and their sister-in-law Bimba's albums of Palm Sunday photographs— photographs in which all the bitterness and worry and aggravations of daily life, including those of the actual occasion, are redeemed in a kind of heroic, candy-tinted afterlife.

Tonight, I have agreed to take Diane shopping at the

supermarket Auchan for her holiday preparations. To me, a trip to the supermarket is a solitary ordeal to be dispatched as quickly as possible. For the Gypsies, it's an outing, and thus demands the number of troops and complexity of planning required to get Hannibal across the Alps.

Twice already that afternoon Diane has called me. "Are you coming? Where are you? You haven't left the house yet?" When my children and I appear, twelve minutes late for our rendezvous, Diane and her niece Tanya are tapping their heels on the sidewalk outside La Fantaisie. Diane is immensely dolled up: black vinyl maxiskirt, lizard platforms, Goth makeup, a couple of pounds of jangling crucifixes, and her hair, newly blonde, tortured into a million African braids—the look that led Garth to describe her as "Anjelica Huston in *The Addams Family.*" Tanya is in her hip-hop tracksuit. "I was about to give up on you," Diane chides me, fondly.

This is the drill. We have to retrieve Kevin and Marlon from Granny Antoinette's, we need to find Moïse, we have to pick up Diane and Linda's brother Daniel. Along the way, a couple more people decide to come along for the ride, such as Nelly, the sweet, spacey, fourteen-year-old daughter of Moïse's brother Jérémie, who is a junkie. Jérémie and Nelly's mother are separated—an event that's rare enough among St. Jacques Gypsies to have bestowed on their children a hushed aura of misfortune. When you are about to meet Nelly, this is what you are told in advance, the way other people might tell you, half-warning, half-gossip, that a child is autistic, or hemophiliac.

Diane hops into the front seat, and we're off. Luckily I'm driving our family station wagon, which unlike my Parisian Renault 5, still has a tape deck. The Gypsies can't stand being without music. Unluckily, my tape collection won't do—Diane flips through it in growing disbelief.

"What's this?" she demands, examining a tape cover portraying a warrior in chain mail.

It's Seamus Heaney's reading of *Beowulf*.

"It's *what*?"

"It's a poet from Garth's country reading a poem."

"A *what*? Fernande, I think you need your head examined."

Even my flamenco classic, Cameron de la Isla, the god of Spanish and hence Perpignan Gypsy musicians, she rejects as fuddy-duddy.

We stop at the rue des Carmes, where Kevin is extracted from playing soccer in the empty lot, and Baby Marlon is buckled into my car seat. Diane disappears. I watch her mount the street, her bad-girl swagger somewhat constrained by ankle-length hobble skirt and stilettos. She is making for the fat, pockmarked cousins sitting on chairs on the sidewalk. Behind me, bottlenecked cars honk.

Finally I get out. "Shall we go?"

Diane is hunting down more acceptable music. First she's hit up Francisquet's semi-retarded granddaughter Nelly (not to be confused with Jérémie's daughter Nelly), who yanks hard on Diane's braids and claims she has no tapes since her machine's broken (Liar, mutters Diane). Nelly likes to treat me as Miss Wheels. Tonight, as usual, she asks me to take her to the beach.

Next it's Jérôme's son Jonathan, who plays keyboard for Los Chiquitos. Diane pounds on the front door of Jérôme's compound, which Jérôme and Sylvie share with their grown children and their children's spouses and children.

It is answered by Jonathan's wife, Vanessa, a pale, impassive "French" girl in long black skirts who has adopted Gypsy ways. How did Jonathan and Vanesssa meet? I once asked Linda.

"She was sixteen; she worked at the bakery where Jonathan stopped for breakfast on his way home from gigs," Linda says. "He started chatting her up. A few free croissants on the side, and there it goes. Gypsies were shocked that Jonathan—a young boy without blemish—was allowed to marry her. If he had a thoroughly Gypsy mentality, he would have married a Gypsy virgin and kept the Frenchwoman on the side, which is what most of the men do."

"Why did she choose to become a Gypsy?" I ask.

"She's still young, eighteen, nineteen. Jonathan's her first love. I imagine when she wakes up, she'll get them out of Jérôme and Sylvie's house, but for now, she has nothing to compare it to."

Later, I meet Vanessa's mother and her mother's boyfriend, hard-drinking bikers in black leather, and I figure that maybe compared with where Vanessa came from, St. Jacques looks orderly, coherent.

In Vanessa's arms is her six-month-old baby. (A couple of months later, she is pregnant with her second. Not an accident, Linda tells me—Vanessa is bent on having a big brood fast, and Jonathan, an easygoing party boy, apparently is willing.)

It's six p.m. and Jonathan is still sleeping off the previous night's concert. Diane, however, has no qualms about waking him so we can have decent music on our drive to the supermarket. I watch Jonathan rise from his mattress on the floor, a long brown boy skinny as a horse, who is wearing only a pair of jaunty red-and-white polka-dot boxer shorts. It's the first time I've seen Jonathan out of dark glasses. He hands over a tape Diane's lent him, yawns, rubs his eyes, and plunges back into sleep as gracefully as a diver leaping into a pool.

St. Jacques music is homemade: you never see a store-bought tape or CD in someone's house. Every piece of music is bootlegged—recorded from live performances of musicians you have never heard of, who play in venues as secret as the cockfight championship. Somebody's cousin was there, and the tape gets passed through a hundred hands and copied, so what reaches you is faded, accidentally spliced, and unutterably delicious, rarefied as an Alan Lomax field recording. Who's this? I ask. It's El Niño de las Lagrimas, it's El Rey de Lebrija, it's Pepitito, a twelve-year-old preacher from Cap d'Agde singing at a first communion party, or a revival meeting in a fairground outside Nîmes, whom you mistake for a girl because his voice hasn't broken. Diane, snapping her fingers, eyes closed, sings along to lyrics attesting to Jesus' love and man's unworthiness. She translates from Gitan to French for me, and makes me sing too.

Next we're supposed to retrieve Moïse from the bar where he plays cards every day with his brother-in-law Samir. But Moïse left his car headlights on all night, so there's a side drama of finding cables and jump-starting his Kyoto off my station wagon. This accomplished, we pile into the two cars.

Last stop is one of Perpignan's downtown shopping-streets—a neighborhood of decayed elegance that's been reclaimed by young couples on a small income, and where Gypsies definitively don't live. Here, in a fourth-floor studio that's been carved out of a turn-of-the-century *hôtel partic-ulier* live Daniel and his wife, Christine.

Daniel is a tall, shambling young man with an air of wry bemusement. Christine, his college sweetheart, a cheerful, down-to-earth Provençale, is eight months pregnant with their first child. Christine is dutiful and affectionate to Daniel's family, but, unlike her cousin-in-law Vanessa, she's firmly anchored in the French mainstream and feels under no compunction to "become" a Gypsy.

Daniel dreams of working in movies or television, but Perpignan is still one of those towns you have to leave if you want to get somewhere—a bargain most Perpignanais consider unacceptable. And for Gypsies, leaving your family is a form of annihilation. Daniel has a job he hates, teaching at a chess academy. His chess tournament trophies are displayed in a glass-fronted cabinet; spread out on the floor, a 50,000-piece jigsaw puzzle—a favorite hobby.

"He's a real intellectual," beams Diane. "Me, I'm an airhead, but Daniel's got a super brain. You'd never take him for a Gypsy, would you?"

Daniel grimaces, embarrassed. This is the running refrain: you'd never take Daniel for a Gypsy. It's true: if his brother Samir goes the full nine yards, Daniel, in Hawaiian shirt, khakis, and only one gold medallion, looks like any second-generation southern Frenchman. He could be Lebanese, Greek, Sephardic, Sicilian—from any number of Mediterranean tribes in which it's taken for granted that young adults prefer to spend their Sundays in loud intimate clan gatherings, and that a man's best friends are his uncle and his brother-in-law.

Daniel doesn't drive: tonight he's hitching a ride in order to buy the week's groceries. Daniel goes in Moïse's car. Kevin, too, switches from my car to the men's. The only male who remains with us (besides my son Theodore) is

Marlon, who at eleven months is still shuffled back and forth across the sexual border.

Our destination, the megasupermarket Auchan, lies on the highway to Spain.

2

Thursday night at Auchan turns out to be a scene. This is when families—a certain kind of family, a little more louche than your Saturday-morning types—do their weekly shopping. The crowd is predominately white working-class French, but there are also young Arab couples with babies, and a cross section of Gypsies—Manush who look like trailer-park French, except that the women wear the Gypsy uniform of long skirts, hair combs, and house slippers, and Andalusian, as well as neighboring St. Jacobites, who look each other over without a word. Saying "hello" is for *paios*.

We proceed down aisles as arctic-antiseptic as a morgue, past high-rises of Cocoa Puffs and low-rises of frozen TV dinners. We are traveling in a gang of ten; if my children and I wander off, Diane shouts us back into the fold.

Even in this mixed crowd, our group is conspicuous for its size and volume. Once again, as when the pizza deliveryman came to Diane's apartment, I find myself on the other side of the looking glass. Even though we aren't doing anything wrong (besides Diane's habit of grabbing food from the shelves and eating it or giving it to the children to eat, before she's bought it), the "French" stare at us sometimes as at something unassimilably exotic, sometimes with outright hostility.

I haven't been looked at like this since I was fifteen and

my best friend, Stephen, was a drag queen from Kentucky who liked to parade along the West Side Highway by night, wearing Elizabethan gowns made out of garbage. Stephen, God bless him, welcomed even the most violent attentions, but Diane and Moïse don't have much choice. Inconspicuousness for most Gypsies just isn't an option.

Later, in the checkout line, we wait behind a white couple in their early forties. The husband, a pinched man in stone-washed jeans and gray Windbreaker, shoulders his wife well away from us, turning around repeatedly to send us poisonous glares. It seems to me you could only stare with such loathing and contempt across a crowded courtroom, at the murderer of your child.

It is exactly one year before the presidential elections of April 2002, in which the National Front leader Jean-Marie Le Pen comes in second, gaining unusually high scores in Roussillon. Decent French people were shocked to learn that so many of their fellow citizens were closet racists, but I had seen too many such glares, heard too many nasty asides from neighbors. Perpignan is the city where, when the young American rock star Ben Harper played on tour, he was turned away from a bar because he was black.

Tonight, I don't bother to place this man's reaction to Gypsies in any wider sociopolitical context, but it does give me a clue as to why St. Jacobites regard all strangers passing through their streets as a potential posse.

Diane, however, like my drag-queen friend Stephen, would rather be glared at than ignored. Anyway, she's on a roll. First she loads up on the week's supplies—coffee and canned food, including canned potatoes, a choice I find particularly egregious, since fresh potatoes grow from Chile to Siberia and even a chimpanzee can peel and boil one, but she urges me, too, to buy some. Then we make our way to the holiday section, where an entire aisle of Palm Sunday—i.e., Easter—baskets are on display.

Almost every basket on offer is branded by an American toy or an American cartoon: there are Action Men eggs in camouflage foil, and Barbie eggs in fuchsia foil, there are Polly Pocket eggs, and Power Ranger eggs, and eggs from this season's Disney movie, which is *Dinosaur.*

These are the gift baskets that will appear on the children's laps in the Palm Sunday photographs in Diane's family album, and hence an elaborate protocol comes into play. The basket must be magnificent, and it must match the child's outfit. Marlon, Diane has decided months ago, will be wearing a white suit, white hat, white socks, and white shoes, so his Palm Sunday basket should be white and blue. Kevin will be, as usual, in red and black. Diane's requirements are extra-complicated, because in addition to the basket on the lap, her children will be bearing aloft palm branches, to which she has to attach sprays of candies light enough not to break the branch. And since my children too will be included in this year's Palm Sunday family photographs, Diane has to guide me into the appropriate choices.

This is where the non-Gypsies once again flunk out. My six-year-old daughter and three-year-old son, faced with half a city block of dehydrogenated cocoa solids and corn syrup, turn out to have opinions and desires just as mulish as Diane's. And their opinions are all wrong. Maud chooses an uncharacteristically modest arrangement consisting of two medium-sized owls made out of orange-colored chocolate.

"An *owl*?" repeats Diane, incredulously. "What's that supposed to mean? No, no, that's way too small: it's got to be *big*. And *pink*. What are you going to dress her in?"

I haven't planned.

"Well, dress her in pink, and get her a Barbie. No, a *big* Barbie. Bigger, bigger, BIGGER!"

We have hit another culture snag. Where I come from, parental love means placing limits on the amount of tooth rot that's acceptable. For Diane, the bigger the candy the bigger the love: a chocolate egg the size of the Parthenon means you love your kid a thousand times more than an egg the size of a ranch house.

Worse is to come. Maud doesn't like Barbie, but guess who does? Her younger brother is *dying* for a chocolate Barbie egg wrapped in glittering hot-pink foil and containing a whole trove of mini-Barbies.

"Pink? Barbie? Him? *T'es folle, ou quoi?* You want your son to grow up to be a faggot?" Diane is frankly revolted by any boy's even for an instant being drawn to the color pink.

Kevin, thank God, has never, never shown such *pédé* propensities, not even when he was three. Theodore is handed instead a chocolate soccer ball and a pair of chocolate soccer shoes, which he doesn't care for. I buy him the pink Barbie egg, too.

3

We are driving home from Auchan—me, Diane, my children. The rest of the gang has stayed on to have dinner at Flunch, the supermarket cafeteria.

The children are falling asleep in the backseat.

"Teach me Gitan," I suggest.

Diane lights up, immensely pleased by the idea.

Moïse has already taught me a couple of phrases, but

I've found that however parrotlike I try to replicate the sounds he's made, nobody can understand the result. There are one or two "French" I know who speak a bit of Gitan, such as Majid Benjagoub, who played b box *rai* for Rumba Mayor and who in turn taught his colleagues some Arabic, but mostly it's unknown territory, for even Catalan speakers profess to have trouble understanding the Gypsy variant, and vice versa.

Diane coaches me. *"Que fem anit?"* (What are we doing tonight?)

I repeat, and she laughs.

"Que fem anit, Fernande? I want to go dancing."

"I want to go to bed."

"Come on, Fernande, let's go dancing, let's go to the Cargo, the Voice, the Fly Bar. I want to have some fun."

We've reached the ring road on the outskirts of Perpignan. We are driving fast along the four-lane boulevard, when suddenly Diane screams, "Reverse! Reverse!"

I pull off the road fast, thinking there's been an accident, but Diane rolls down the window, and shouts, joyously, *"Putain!* What the fuck are you doing here, you little bitch?"

She jumps out of the car. What she's spotted is a young woman who is dragging a plaid wheeled shopping caddy along the highway. The woman is about thirty; she's peroxide blonde, with no front teeth, crackhead gaunt and cavernous.

"Where you going, bitch?"

"Bitch" is headed to catch a bus home.

"We'll give you a lift," Diane pronounces.

I grumble: it's late, I'm beat, the kids have got school tomorrow.

"Come on, Fernande, she lives just around the corner."

I grudgingly consent. In fact, the woman lives way out nowhere, across the river and past the fairground, in some back-end suburban wilderness I didn't know existed.

Diane chatters avidly all the way; "Bitch" is rather hesitant, delicate in her replies. I struggle to follow, because although Diane's speaking French, she's speaking fast and rough in a burry gobble of slang.

Diane is complaining about some woman whom she's just discovered *still* keeps framed photographs of Moïse on her bedroom dresser, and even though the woman's assured Diane that these are old photos she simply hasn't gotten around yet to dismantling (something Diane can halfway believe, since the woman's place is a filthy rat hole), still, her not having removed the photographs of Moïse is nonetheless a blatant breach of the treaty she and Diane had agreed to.

After we drop off "Bitch" outside her building, Diane turns to me, immensely amused. "Fernande, you'll never believe who that was. *That was Moïse's mistress.*"

"That blonde with no teeth?"

"Yeah, you'd think at least he could have picked someone with *more* teeth than me." She roars with laughter. "He could have picked someone *better* than me, wouldn't you think? She's not even any younger. And you know what?" She leans toward me, and reveals in a hushed tone: *"She's not really blonde."*

So in fact, the woman with the photographs of Moïse on her bedroom dresser of whom Diane was complaining is the woman she was addressing.

Diane explains to me that Moïse and this chick were together a long time, five years or so. "I never would have known, if her husband hadn't come and told me. When I found out, I took Kevin with me up to Paris; we moved in with my cousins. But Moïse came and found us. I said, Live with her, marry her, I don't really care, but Moïse said, No, it's you I want to be with. I guess you must think it's strange I'm so friendly with her, but believe me, I've beaten her up already. (Not nearly as bad as I beat up Mo.) And why should I take it out on her, poor fool, when it was my husband who was the shit?

"You think I'm happy, Fernande, but I'm desperately unhappy. I spend all my life crying, crying.

"That's why I never go out anymore: I know I'm going to hear something bad. I'd rather stay at home with my children, *tranquille*."

4

On Sunday afternoon Alastair, Maud, Theodore, and I drive over to Diane and Moïse's apartment on Boulevard Aristide Briand. We take two cars since Moïse's Kyoto is now officially on the blink.

There's been plenty of domestic drama between Thursday night and Sunday afternoon. On Friday night, Moïse once again didn't come home. It's noon on Saturday, Diane is in tears—he still isn't home. By two p.m., still no Moïse. (Maybe he's attending an adult literacy course, my husband, Alastair, suggests, helpfully.) Saturday night, Moïse finally shows up, explaining that he was with Jeannot the previous night, and then went directly to an all-day cockfight. Diane is hugely relieved by this explanation.

When we arrive on Sunday afternoon, the Espinas family is playing gin rummy. Diane and Moïse play, Diane wins; Moïse and Kevin play, Kevin is caught cheating; Diane and Kevin play, Diane wins a hundred francs from him. Moïse teaches Alastair to play, Alastair plays with Moïse, then with Kevin. Diane, supervising, catches both Moïse and Kevin cheating.

It takes an hour or so for Diane to get dressed.

Today it's her sister, Linda, who's out of sorts. Even though it was Linda's idea that we all spend Palm Sunday together, now she's in a pissy mood, and doesn't want to come. Linda often gets in a sulk about family outings: they are pay-your-own-way occasions, which remind her that although the other women in her family live off a combination of welfare and their husband's "black" earnings, she—as she likes to tell you, in her jaunty, schoolgirl English—has "no husband, no money," and works a low-paying public-sector job in order to support her two children.

Once I've coaxed Linda into coming up to the mountains with us (big mistake, as she fumes in silence all night), there's a new hitch in the form of Linda's Kurdish ex-boyfriend, Erkan, who, although remarried, with a new family, is still something of a stalker.

Erkan has just called, presumably from the corner, and Moïse, who likes stirring trouble, has "accidentally" let slip that Linda and their son Mickaël are heading up to the border town of Le Perthus for a party. Linda dives into my car, ducking herself and Mickaël down, just as Erkan rings her doorbell. "Go, go, go!" she urges me.

Unfortunately, I get the gears confused and, with a roar of the engine, zoom top-speed *backward* past the doorway where Erkan waits. "You really should learn how to drive someday," she suggests, squawking with terrified laughter.

This is the last time Linda consents to be driven by me, and she sits white-knuckled all the way up to Le Perthus. Diane sits in the back loyally protesting that she *loves* my driving, it doesn't scare her a bit, she thinks it's a riot even when the passenger door flies open on a roundabout.

Moïse, in the front car, proves as nervous a passenger as his sister-in-law. When, thanks to multiple cell phones, we reconnoiter at a rest area out of town, I discover that Moïse is now driving our station wagon, and Alastair is in the passenger seat. I stare at my husband, flabbergasted; he smiles back beatifically. When I see Moïse behind the wheel of our gleaming new Peugeot 306—which my husband is fanatical about not letting anybody touch who isn't insured to drive it—I appreciate the full nature of Moïse's charm, which is to convey a solid, man-among-men reliability.

Moïse, who likes to drive at forty kilometers an hour *max* and puts on the hand brake at every stoplight, even on a flat surface, avoids the superhighway that gets you to the border in fifteen minutes. Crawling along the small twisty back roads, past thermal spas and Romanesque monasteries, we eventually arrive at Le Perthus.

5

Le Perthus, half in France, half in Spain, is a honky-tonk discount town. Every weekend, it's stuffed with busloads of French stocking up on cheap cigarettes, liquor, videos. It's an outing for retired people, an Atlantic City without gambling.

"What shall we do?" asks Diane.

It's a blue-and-gold spring afternoon, but the Tramontane is howling. With the wind at 125 kilometers an hour, we don't stand a chance of photographing the children outside. The restaurant doesn't open until seven. We have an hour to kill.

We shop. Hauling Marlon's stroller up and downstairs, we cruise from floor to floor of cut-rate department stores offering lighting, furniture, electronics, household goods of a penny-arcade crappiness, along with touristy "Spanish" knickknacks, such as polka-dotted flamenco dresses in all sizes from toddler to mammoth. We check out the music section, which—aimed at retirees—is all tapes, consisting either of traditional Catalan *coblas* or Gypsy crooners from the '60s, including the father and the uncle of Moïse's Tekameli colleague Julio Bermudez.

We buy presents for the children. Diane, for whom presents must be expensive, brand-name, status-conferring, once again is baffled by the dull utilitarianism of what my children pick—a compass for Maud, a flashlight for Theodore. There's extra amusement when she asks me what I've bought my son, and I reply, confusing *torche* and *torchon,* "A dish towel," thus confirming her suspicion that I want the kid to be a *pédé.*

We head on to dinner. The restaurant, which is on the Spanish side, is at first sight uninviting: a self-serve cafeteria with harsh strip lighting, empty at seven p.m. except for one extremely drunk waiter.

Moïse, abstemious unless he's expressly on a binge, orders a half-bottle of red wine for the men. (The women, by St. Jacques tradition, are not allowed to drink.) I drink beer, with which Diane surreptitiously cuts her lemonade.

When the food arrives—enormous platters of paella—it's cheap and delicious, but something's wrong. I try to make conversation with Moïse, Alastair tries to talk to Linda, but everybody is uncomfortable. Finally, Diane set things right. From her end of the table, she shouts, "Fernande, come sit by me! I'm all alone with the men!"

I move my place to Diane's end, and now there is a general shift. Moïse, with immense relief, summons Alastair and

Kevin to his side of the table. But the reshuffle is not yet complete: even three-year-old Theodore and five-year-old Mickaël, at Moïse's insistence, are brought to join the men. The rightful order established, everyone can now relax, and conversations become voluble, intimate. The men talk cock-fights and music, the women talk about their pregnancies, and the children boast about which one's got more Poké-mon cards.

We laugh, it's fun, and the original point of the occasion—photographing the children in their Palm Sunday best, posed on the parapet overlooking the plain of Roussil-lon, each bearing candy-laden palm branches and a giant Barbie or Action Man basket—seems to be slipping away. From time to time, someone will mention taking the photo-graphs, and someone else says, Later. Somewhere along the way, Moïse realizes he's lost his camera. I suggest he borrow mine, but everybody agrees it's too windy, and by now the children's Palm Sunday finery is drenched in ketchup and pork fat.

Instead, I take my own pictures of our celebration. It's years later now, and I am looking at these photographs, which are so different from the posed frozen serenity of the Palm Sunday photographs in Diane's or Bimba's family albums.

The table is littered with Coke bottles, sausage butts, empty cigarette packs, scarlet crayfish, the children's already broken trinkets. The guests sprawl like revelers in a seventeenth-century Flemish tavern scene. Tanya, head back, laughs so wide you can see the roof of her mouth, while her sparkly-eyed kid brother grapples her. Moïse unrolls a wad of twenty-franc notes, one Mephistophelian eyebrow hooked. Diane hugs me tight. Linda, eyes blazing, is arched like a cat about to spring. Everyone looks drunk, rumpled, and electri-cally alive.

Back home that night, under a sea of stars, Alastair is still wired. It's his first night with the Gypsies, and I see that he too finds them very, very exciting company: maddening, a little goes a long way, but exciting, nonetheless.

Chapter Twelve

1

Diane operates on a feast-or-famine economy. There are months when Moïse isn't getting any gigs, and the house phone and cell phones are cut off, and bank accounts frozen on account of checks that have bounced, and Diane says she can't even afford diapers for the baby, and at such times, her mother steps in with groceries and hand-me-down clothes.

But even in their lean months, Diane still manages to find Kevin a back-to-school knapsack that costs four times more than any knapsack anybody else has ever seen, and to feel guilty because she can't buy him the cell phone that goes in the matching cell-phone cover. Why?

Because Gypsies, who have no older prudential ethic to fall back on, for whom it's always been a point of pride not to worry about the next day's meal, are peculiarly vulnerable to the smallpox of consumerism, in which people are persuaded to express their love for their children through the acquisition of crappy goods they can't afford, a substitution which applies to everything from Christmas toys to afternoon snacks.

Dr. Morcrette, my pediatrician friend, tells me, "The Gypsy mothers have lost their old culinary ways, the good *escudellas* of meat and potatoes, and instead have this guilty mentality of buying their children 'the best,' and because processed food is more expensive than home cooked, it must be better. I see these children who help themselves freely to kitchen cabinets stuffed with chips and candy, babies who are given Coca-Cola in their bottles instead of milk. I say, You want your son to be healthy? Cut the Coke. But he asks for it! Yes, and if he wants to hang himself, you'll give him a rope?"

The feeling of unworthiness if you don't spend money you don't have on junk you don't need is not peculiar to Gypsies: the American economy is based on this particular pathology. When, after September 11th, Americans lined up to offer their blood, their blankets, their free labor, the president of the United States told them the best way to fulfill their patriotic duty was by spending.

But people whose sense of self-worth is not strong, who feel stigmatized by strangers, are especially vulnerable to the lure of consumption.

The most glaring example is a woman whom the French press called "Mère Noël" (Mrs. Santa Claus).

Mère Noël was a twenty-eight-year-old mother of seven children, living in a trailer in a campground on the outskirts of Lyons, trying to get by on welfare benefits of five dollars a day. Just before Christmas, Mère Noël took her children to the supermarket. Ambushed by glittery, twittering Christmas displays at every corner, by the Barbie pool-party sets, the *Star Wars* walkie-talkies her children were begging for, she loaded her shopping cart with Christmas toys (a whopping 3,892 francs, or 800 dollars' worth!) and tried to make a run for it. She would have succeeded, too, had she not been ratted on by a fellow-customer, an unidentified toady who should rot in hell.

The following January, Mère Noël was sentenced to six months in prison and five years' deprivation of civil rights—rights which include the ability to hold a bank account. Most pathetic of all was Mère Noël's wooden guilelessness, her inability to see herself as a victim of predatory marketing aimed at those least able to afford the goods being hawked. (Poor single mothers have little choice but to bring their children along to the supermarket; poor single mothers are the ones most liable to let their kids watch long bouts of TV cartoons, which are jam-packed with ads for toys without which your child is jesuitical in persuading you his life is not worth living.)

Asked if she has anything to say in her own defense, Mère Noël, hanging her head, volunteers that she knows what she did was "bad." Asked by reporters if she doesn't feel her prison sentence is unjust, Mère Noël gives the standard bureaucratic response that is drilled into every French citizen asking to be treated as a human being: if she weren't punished for stealing, "then everybody would go and do it."

Mère Noël is the somnambulistic precursor to the anti-capitalist movement's Don't Buy days, to the Barcelona collective Yo Mango (I steal), whose members parade the streets in clothes ripped off from chain stores.

But Mère Noël will never make it to the logical next step of her act of consumer disobedience. Mère Noël, because she feels so "bad," wants to be good. Mère Noël will be a model prisoner. All Mère Noël wants is a chance to earn enough money to acquire licitly the goods her children crave.

"What did Alastair get you for Mother's Day?" Diane asks me. (Alixter, she calls him.)

"Nothing!"

"Nothing?" she repeats, shocked.

"I'm not his mother," I point out, laughing.

"You are the mother of his children," Diane says, severely. She genuinely thinks less well of my husband for this omission.

She leads me to her bedroom closet, where she reveals to me Moïse's Mother's Day presents to her. Row upon row of maxiskirts—black vinyl, camouflage, snakeskin, each a strip of flimsily sewn synthetic material. She shows me the labels, one after another: Morgan, Morgan, Morgan (a local French brand).

"Only the top brand names," she grins, proudly.

If Diane is dressed in head-to-toe Morgan, she figures, maybe next time the bouncer will let her in to Boca Boca.

2

By local standards, Diane and Moïse live well. Moïse earns a decent income from his concerts, in addition to getting social security when he's not working. Diane receives all the payments available to single mothers, since she and Moïse are not legally married, as well as the housing benefits and child benefits, including subsidized after-school programs and holiday camps, for which low-income families are eligible.

Diane and Moïse rent a comfortable, modern, centrally heated two-bedroom apartment in downtown Perpignan that is well equipped with dishwasher, washer-dryer, microwave, two TVs, a VCR, and two stereos. Diane takes the kids up to

Paris every other year to visit relatives, and when it's Marlon's or Kevin's birthday, she throws a party for thirty without thinking twice.

In St. Jacques terms, Diane and Moïse qualify as rich, but they live in a culture of poverty. Tekameli signs a contract with Sony, but Moïse and Diane remain "poor," just as Diane's parents owned two Paris restaurants and yet still lived in a high-rise project in the *banlieues*. In our village, the local hero is a man who won a Lotto jackpot, bought a Ferrari for himself and a new villa for his aged parents, but is praised for otherwise living "exactly as before."

Diane and Moïse would still be poor, even if they were millionaires, because even in today's moneyocracy, money doesn't equal class or power. They would be poor, because they don't have the ambition or the patience or the know-how that can solidify your gains, translate wealth into less transient goods such as education or health care or political influence. They don't even have access to the institutions that help you hang on to your money, let alone make it grow. (In an Istanbul shantytown, I once met a woman who, with her husband, had made a fortune in Germany and who now owned a car showroom in a fancy suburb of the city. The car dealership was doing fine, but they were still facing bankruptcy, because they were paying three-hundred-percent interest on the loan they'd taken out, since no mainstream bank would have them.) Mental poverty has its costs: Moïse will probably die a little younger than he should, not because he can't get hold of a good doctor, but because he's still subject to the premodern conviction that it's going to the doctor that kills you.

Tekameli's next CD could become a worldwide hit, and Moïse would still find himself in a Barcelona police station for trying to sell a plane ticket he has no proof of buying, because what the Jean Moulin teacher slyly referred to as "the realm of paper" will always be foreign to him. He can make a million dollars, but he can't count them.

Which is why Moïse feels safer, more *tranquille*, at home in his own neighborhood, slowly navigating the snaky rivulets of Little Money Street and Eel Street in his aquamarine Kyoto, with days of playing cards in Le Rugbyman with his brother-in-law Samir, nights of "enjoying nature" in the strip mall of Rivesaltes.

Moïse and Diane have left St. Jacques, but they've only moved across the street.

3

My own lifelong love of Europe as a place that's not necessarily more sophisticated than America, but definitely dirtier and more pungent, has always been bound up with Gypsies.

For centuries, non-Gypsies like me have envied Gypsies their seeming freedom, have dreamed of following the open road, roasting a plucked hedgehog over a campfire, sleeping under the stars, learning to riding bareback: no school, no bedtime, no baths. ("What care I for my goose-feather bed, / with the sheets turned down so bravely-o? / For tonight I will sleep in a cold open field / Along with the raggle-taggle Gypsies-o!") But over the years, it is "our" lives that have become increasingly mobile and venturesome, while theirs— pinched between their own tribal prohibitions and decades of government restrictions on nomadism—are ever more confined.

In the tiny troglodytic hamlets of Roussillon's Cerdagne—

the high Pyrenean plateau which, since the days of cavemen hunting mastodons, has been a strategic pass from France to Spain—people's first language is Catalan. A blind church-warden in the village of Llo tells me, "It wasn't till they called our fathers to fight in the First War that we found out we were French."

Diane still hasn't fully found out that she's "French," but nowadays the French aren't anonymous officers summoning you to die in muddy northern ditches: the "French" are college-educated women who drive their Fiat Puntos to the office, women who, like Diane and Linda's friend Isabelle, take night classes in anthropology and belly dancing, and go to look at Roman ruins in Tunisia for their Easter vacation.

I sometimes wonder how I can share some of my freedom with Diane, but my use of it strikes her as deadly dull. I ask her to come along on my sorties, but she's baffled by my idea of fun. She knows she's a prisoner, but if she had my chances, she certainly wouldn't choose to sit in front of a computer screen all day, or, for a treat, go to an Iranian movie about earthquake relief. Diane teases me that I've been "spotted" in the street with Garth Beattie from the Casa. I say, Yeah, we were going to a conference together.

"A conference?"

"A teachers' conference about Gypsy education," I explain. Diane stares at me, frankly appalled. I think she would almost rather believe, for my sake, that Garth and I were emerging from the rent-by-the-hour hotel on the rue des Remparts Saint-Jacques than that we were actually up to something so mind-numbingly, so inexplicably tedious.

Gypsy difference remains formidable. But what does it mean to be a sedentary Gypsy—a Gypsy living, for example, in a government housing project on the outskirts of a Western European city, whose days are spent lining up in a welfare office, waiting to fill out forms?

The French Gypsy filmmaker Tony Gatlif captures this modern-day reversal in his movie *Swing,* in which an upper-middle-class boy from a comfortable northern French suburb falls in love with a Gypsy girl living in a nearby housing project. When the boy's errant mother whisks him away for a summer of Greek island–hopping, the Gypsy-girl says, wistfully, "I've never in my life left the project."

Garth's wife, Pascale, remarks, "Apollinaire said that Gypsies have no history, only geography. And today, no geography, either."

The Gypsies of St. Jacques, having recovered from heroin addiction and AIDS, are now suffering from terminal boredom.

4

Imagine a middle-class family in Roussillon with the same annual income as Moïse and Diane. This family might feel pinched, yet they would be sustained by cultural assumptions and expectations to which Moïse and Diane have no access.

Take my friends Marc and Caroline. Their grandparents were farmworkers, but their fathers each acquired the professional qualifications that launched them into the French suburban middle class. Marc and Caro, nostalgic for their rural roots, have chosen hippiedom. Marc's a carpenter, and Caroline does odd jobs picking grapes or painting houses or helping immigrant children with their homework. They rent a tumble-down house in the Pyrenean foothills which they're fixing up, in exchange for rock-bottom rent, and they have one daughter, to whom they read books borrowed from the library and whom they take to the children's theater festivals that tour Roussillon. When they need a little money, Marc goes down to Barcelona to do custom cabinetry on boats, and they get by, he tells me, on $12,000 a year.

A family can live well off $12,000 a year in Roussillon, as long as nobody drinks or gets into debt. On weekends, they camp in the mountains and swim in the hot springs. In the summer, they drive their Deux Chevaux to Morocco for a month, and sleep in the desert. When you go to their house for dinner, there are tomatoes from their garden, Caroline's baked a cake, and you listen to Django Reinhardt till three in the morning.

Marc and Caroline aren't poor. They don't have much money, but most people in Roussillon don't have much either, and the sense of poverty is comparative. Television, which as we've seen in St. Jacques exposes repressed women to a world of freedom and opportunities, also makes poor people feel poorer. For Diane, her sense of poverty is triggered by a stream of brand-name goods which she's itching to buy, which make her feel inadequate when she can't, and quickly dissatisfied when she does.

5

In the Danish writer Peter Hoeg's novel *Borderliners*, which takes place in a sadistic boarding school, a boy is given a psychological test. He is shown Aesop's fable in which the grasshoppers, who have sung all summer while the ants toiled, in winter come to the ants begging for help, and are told, "You sang? Well, now you may dance." The boy is asked the moral of this fable. In his head, he thinks, The moral is, Ants are not kind. But he knows this is not the answer his masters are waiting for, or on which the world is predicated, so he tries to come up with the expected response. The right answer is harsh, self-righteous, punitive.

There are Gypsies who have broken free of the grasshopper code and joined the scrimp-and-save middle classes. Diane's mother, Antoinette, who got a factory job at sixteen, knows you only get ahead by hard work. Diane's sister, Linda, too, is a striver. She missed her own chance, because of getting pregnant too young. But Linda's daughter, Tanya, whose father runs his own business in Paris, will go on to college and practice a profession, because both parents have given her a sense of all there is to be done in the world, besides gawk at store windows.

Diane has managed to protect her children from the specific stigmata of St. Jacques Gypsydom, without freeing them from poverty's short sights. Diane knows enough to make her son Kevin go to school, but not enough to show him what school might lead to, in part because Perpignan is a town on the margins, where there are hurdy-gurdy players and seamstresses and knife-grinders and public scribes, but no "professionals." This is a place you have to leave early if you want to achieve something, or else suffer the kind of career drop peculiar to Soviet-era dissidents.

There is no one to tell Kevin, You could be an architect, you could be a lawyer, you could be a marine biologist, you could go to Toulouse and make high-precision tools for Aerospatiale or work as a sous-chef at the Hôtel de l'Opera.

Diane sees the doctor every day of her life, but she has never thought that one of her sons might study medicine.

Gypsies get sick, but they don't become doctors. The closest they get is being Pentacostalist healers.

Gypsies don't have alarm clocks. Gypsies aren't even supposed to play chess. Gypsies rarely get past Little Money Street.

6

Life in Roussillon is closer to inner-city soap opera than to one's image of the south of France. When your neighbor drops by to recount the village gossip, it's a tangle of incest, AIDS, suicide attempts, drug addiction, children getting taken into foster care—sad histories of generational decline, in which the grandfather was a communist blacksmith up north, the parents skilled factory workers, and the children who've come south to enjoy the sun live off summer jobs as cleaners in a campground.

In many ways, our Roussillon neighbors subscribe to a global culture which is American-generated. My children's schoolmates, like St. Jacques Gypsies, are named Jason, Ryan, Tiffany, Megan, names their parents can't properly pronounce, any more than American parents can properly pronounce "Michelle" or "Denise." The better-off families, who mostly have migrated from the industrial north, live in gated communities called Malibu Village or Le Honolulu that have been raised on land that ten years ago was orchards or fishermen's huts. The kids watch dubbed *Rugrats* and *Scooby-Doo*, the parents watch Bruce Willis DVDs and take Prozac. (French people have the world's highest per capita consumption of antidepressants.) They go to Tex-Mex restaurants for a night out, the richer kids have birthday parties at McDonald's, and shop for hip-hop or surfer gear at the mall. Like Gypsies, they are brand-name obsessed, and believe a strip of nylon with the label MORGAN is worth a hundred euros, while the same strip of nylon labeled TEX is only worth thirty.

It's easy to conclude that people here have adopted the worst of American culture—junk food, designer drugs, rootlessness, divorce, a television set that like the fluorescent lights in prison stays on day and night, fending off the wolves of reflection or intimacy. But crucial differences remain. Among the people I meet in Roussillon, there is an inherited Mediterranean culture, a conception of "the good life," which is in many ways antithetical to the reigning free-market ethic. Instead of ingenuity and enterprise, what people value is neighborliness, respect, stability, leisure. Money or success, perhaps because there isn't much of either, come far below. Ambition scarcely figures. "Individualism" is a dirty word, signifying a me-first piggishness. Work is not an end in itself: most people in Roussillon would agree with Gypsies that you'd be nuts to work a job that paid less than unemployment. Here it's considered proper for men as well as women to put family life before career: a man who leaves for the office at dawn and comes home just in time to give his children a good-night kiss isn't thought to be making a sacrifice, but a selfish mistake.

What's been your biggest culture shock, Dr. Morcrette asks me. Lunch, I reply. Every day, from noon till two, our children are sent home from school in the expectation that at least one of their parents will leave work, so that the entire family can sit down together to a hot cooked meal. (There's a cafeteria for children whose parents work away from home, but such children consider themselves hardship cases.)

If France were ever taken over by a ruling junta of Free Marketers, the first thing the incoming dictators would do is abolish lunch. Because it is clearly intolerable that any developed Western capitalist economy should close down for two hours in the middle of the working day, while parents join their children at home for a three-course meal. (In Perpignan, the biggest traffic jam isn't in the morning or evening, but at twelve and two.)

But for most people I know in Roussillon, lunch is a necessary brake on ambition, a reminder of what really counts. "Family" is not the opposite of "adult"—i.e., pornographic—but the one real thing in a world of shadows.

7

I meet Jeannot Soler at Le Rugbyman, the Bas Vernet bar which today is empty except for an overweight white barman who is scarfing down a Big Mac. Most of the compass points in Jeannot's life lie in the Vernet *banlieues*—down the block from Le Rugbyman is the Palais des Expositions, where his wedding—with a thousand guests, including a delegation from Sony—took place.

We get into Jeannot's BMW. He wants to show me his new apartment and introduce me to his wife, Incarnacion, a tall, languorous Andalusian with eyes the color of green olives, and their eighteen-month-old baby. "Write in your book his name is Antonio, I want my son immortalized," Jeannot says. But first he's got an errand in town.

Jeannot swerves across the river and heads into St. Jacques, blasting Cameron de la Isla songs from the '70s, along with new-wave rumba. We cruise along the rue Llucia, searching for a North African pastry store, but the shops are all barred shut for lunch. Finally we spot one that's open.

Three years later—after I've left Roussillon—this same tea shop became infamous as the place where a French Algerian man named Mohammed Bey-Bachir was trapped and bludgeoned to death by a mob of Gypsies, one of whom he'd threatened for trying to steal his car radio. This lynching set off city-wide riots by Perpignan Arabs and brought to the surface all the underlying bitternesses between Muslims and their Gypsy neighbors. Today, however, the fragile peace is still intact. Jeannot dips inside the pastry shop—a pileup of cars behind honking splenetically—and emerges with a box of baklava.

"For my sister-in-law," he explains, with a wink. "She's pregnant; she's got a craving for Arab sweetmeats. Why it's always me, and not my brother, who's got to answer her cravings is another question. . . ."

When we arrive at the project of Haut Vernet, he shouts up at a window, and the mother-to-be appears to claim her cakes.

This project is where Jeannot was born and raised. His parents, his grandparents, his *tontons,* his *tatas,* his cousins, his sisters and three brothers all live here, as well as the friends he grew up with. Out back is his brother the pastor, who is fiddling with the engine of a red Peugeot 205. "My brothers and I pooled together to buy our dad that car for Father's Day," Jeannot explains. "We paid ten thousand francs for it. It's the first car he's had in his life."

To Jeannot, family is an unmitigated blessing. There is no sense among Gypsies—or anybody else I meet here—that young people might want to get out on their own, to assert their independence or autonomy: it's a hard, menacing world, you need all the support you can get.

"With my family here, I'm *tranquille,*" says Jeannot. "When I'm on the road, I don't have to worry about my wife and son's safety."

Jeannot, like Moïse, insists that he "wants to go far," but he places strict limits on his ambitions. He talks to me about the Gipsy Kings, who come from one of the most prominent Catalan Gypsy clans in the area.

"The Gipsy Kings were great musicians, but they blew it because they were too greedy for money, they lost their family *feeling.*" (He uses the English word.) "We want to succeed, not just to be rich, but so that we can take care of our parents, look after our own. A grand here, a grand there, and then home, *tranquille,* to our families."

"Nicolas Reyes left his wife and kids, and went to live in Paris with a *paia.* This was not a normal girl you might pick up on the street or in a nightclub, this was a prostitute *de luxe* who spent all Nicolas's money and then left him."

Today, you can find Nicolas Reyes sitting on the steps of his trailer in the Camargue, a bitter man complaining that Gypsy life has gone to the dogs because young people no longer listen to their elders, and husbands let their wives run around in the streets.

"I want a normal life," says Jeannot. "I want to do my work and come home at night. Our own lives first, the music after. If not, your wife and kids are truly fucked."

When I first encountered Tekameli's music, I wanted to help make them world famous. I kept telling Moïse about record executives I knew in London or New York who might be able to sign them up, if Sony fell through. Moïse, though polite, evinced little interest.

My assumption was that Moïse thought I was bluffing, that a woman who spent her time hanging out in shopping malls with Diane couldn't have much in the way of cosmopolitan pull. It took me a couple more years of living in Roussillon before I saw his point. For Moïse, "real life" did not take place in boardrooms in Rockefeller Center. Of all the glittering favors I claimed to have at my disposal, there was only one thing I could do for Moïse he considered worth doing, and that was find him the little plot of land on which to keep a fighting cock.

8

To the French people I know, America is the permanently self-regenerating creator of myths, heroes, cultic objects they cherish, whether it's Indian chiefs, Converse All Stars, diners with jukeboxes in each booth, or Kurt Cobain.

They want to consume American culture the way Americans want to consume sushi or tacos, but they don't want to *be* American, because being American implies a willful amnesia, a loss of inherited familial and societal values, a preference for individualism over solidarity. Perhaps because they are southerners, Roussillonais, Gypsies included, express a stronger kinship to Latin Americans, who are perceived as having similar attitudes toward family, religion, sexual roles, sickness and death, a similar taste in music and sports, including cockfights.

When people in Roussillon ask me about America, they are usually telling me about America, a country in which parents work three jobs and still don't have health insurance for their children, in which mentally retarded boys sit on death row, or a Louisiana home-owner shoots dead a Japanese exchange student for mistakenly ringing his doorbell on Halloween, and is acquitted.

It seems to them a lonely, dangerous place of extremes, a

place that's uncivilized, unsafe, simultaneously soul-deadening and thrilling, and that represents the ultimate challenge to one's courage and endurance. I have never felt so nonchalantly brave solely on account of the color of my passport.

During my years in Roussillon, I have only met one person who has lived in America and who thinks things were done better there, and she gave me quite a chill. She was a rich divorcée who lamented how in French supermarkets, you were obliged to bag your own groceries, while in the U.S., "boys" delivered them to your door—a line of observation I was otherwise accustomed to hearing from corporate wives who had been stationed in the Third World.

Has America really become, more than welfare-state Europe, a country in which the comfort of the middle classes rests on rickshaw labor, on a workforce of clandestine coolies toiling to send minimum-wage dollars home to their families? Is Europe any better?

Chapter Thirteen

1

One day, my friend Alice asks me to accompany her to the police station. Her ex-boyfriend has broken into her apartment, robbed her, and beaten her black and blue. It's not the first time he's beaten her, or used her cash card to raid her bank account, or forged checks in her name, but it's the first time she's been willing to report it to the police. She's a strong-minded, muscular young woman who feels sorry for people who behave badly, and it hurts her self-respect to think of herself as having been abused.

I am wearing a navy-blue dress and a string of pearls: I'm familiar with French officialdom's brisk polish, and I want to look respectable in order to add credibility to Alice's story. What awaits us, however, is the same torpor and abandon that pervades so many of Perpignan's official spaces—the airport, the hospital, the central post office. Places that make you think, I am not in the provinces, I am in a colony whose former rulers have unceremoniously fled, but neither are the victorious guerrillas anywhere to be seen.

It's 9:30 a.m. It's already broiling hot. And there are

already so many people waiting to talk to the police that the crowd has spilled through the doors and down the outside staircase. Most people are sitting on the bare cement. Some people crouch on their haunches. Some people sit on a newspaper. A couple of provident women have brought their own chairs. The crowd is almost exclusively Arab and black African, and there is an atmosphere of amused disgust almost amounting to gaiety.

We sit on the cement floor in the baking sun for two hours, waiting to see a policeman.

A tall, gangly Moroccan boy beside us strikes up a conversation. He comes from Tangier, and he's in his third year of economics at the University of Perpignan. He wants to become an accountant. There are so few qualified accountants back in Morocco, he tells us, that you can freelance for fifteen different companies, but you need bribe money and connections to get the work.

In the summers, he works as a cook at Canet Plage. Two days ago, he bought a car so he could drive back and forth to his summer job, but yesterday he backed his new car into a van—his fault entirely, he explains ruefully, which is why he is at the police station.

"Will you stay in France after you finish your studies?" I ask.

No way, he replies. Of course, there are much greater opportunities here in France, but he's going back to Tangier, because all his family is there.

To this boy, family is an irreplaceable resource. You'd no more live in a country where you didn't have your family than you'd build a house on land without water.

The Moroccan boy asks Alice, who has recently dropped out of the same university, what she means to do next, but she is uncharacteristically silent. I'm not sure whether it's because her ex-boyfriend who beat her up is also North African, perhaps leaving her with a more general reluctance to strike up an acquaintance with young Arab males, or because the experience has so shaken her up that she no longer knows what she wants to do.

When it's our turn, we are shown to the desk of a brawny Catalan. The policeman doesn't ask any questions; he simply looks over Alice's medical certificate, in which her doctor has claimed that her injuries kept her home from work for two days. This document is called an ITT *(Interromption Temporaire de Travail),* and it's the only piece of evidence that counts in an assault case: a joke in an area where a hangover's an acceptable excuse for staying home from work.

The policeman sighs, blows out his cheeks. "Two days off work? Frankly, that's nothing. It's got to be eight days, at least. You might as well tear up this piece of paper. Why couldn't he have written eight days?"

I'm appalled. This is the *second* time Alice's former boyfriend has beaten her up, and the third time he's kited a check in her name. What's to stop the guy from coming back?

"If he comes back, get the doctor to write you a decent ITT."

2

I am sitting with my daughter, Maud, in the Patisserie Sales, where we go for tea every Wednesday after her music lesson. Sales is an old-fashioned pastry store that's run by a lively young Portuguese woman named Christina, who has long, glossy black hair.

The bakery is on the Avenue Foch, the commercial drag of St. Mathieu, the Gypsy-Arab-migrant-worker-drug-dealer neighborhood bordered by the synagogue, the art college, and the conservatory: a neighborhood of Artful Dodgers, evidently, since Christina keeps the Popsicle freezer by the front door padlocked. Today the only other customer in the Sales is a Moroccan who lives alone above the bakery and comes in every day for his coffee and cake. He has been in France for thirty years, he tells me. In the summers, he goes "home" to see his family. He is a courtly man who has retained the formal manners of *"là-bas"*: he addresses Christina as if she were a favorite daughter-in-law.

The next customer is an art student in white leather zip-up boots and a crew cut. The Moroccan asks after the art student's boyfriend and daughter, and wants to know when they're going to have another baby.

"Never!"

"You must have more children, life without children is empty."

The art student doesn't think she's ready to have another. One's tough enough.

"How can she have a second when her three-year-old *still* won't sleep through the night?" Christina interjects.

The man raises his hands in a gesture of acceptance and politely desists. "God, too, is only One."

When he leaves the shop, Christina calls after him, "Remember our date!"

Tomorrow they are going to the tribunal to testify against a robber who tried to empty the till: the old man, who was passing by, held him down until the police came.

The following Wednesday, Maud and I go as usual for tea at Patisserie Sales. The day is September 12, 2001. Christina is outraged by what "They" have done to my twin towers.

"Have you noticed how there aren't any Arabs in the streets of Perpignan today?" she demands, with vengeful glee. "No, *They* know better than to show their faces outside!"

3

Young Arab men in Perpignan recount to you their daily humiliations. Bouncers turn you away from bars; landladies will say, with perfect freedom, that yes, they've got an apartment free, but they don't rent to Arabs. A recent report to the French group SOS Racisme showed that banks tell the same applicant the job's taken when his name is Farid and offer it to him when he reapplies as Thibault.

"I talked to a young man who works in a bakery," Mouloud Aounit, president of the French antidiscrimination movement MRAP, tells me, "He gets up at five every morning, works twelve hours a day. 'Saturday night,' he says, 'I want to go out to a club: they won't let me in.' Laughing ruefully, 'They don't even want my money.' That's the score: if an Arab dresses decently, has a nice car, he's got to be a drug dealer."

Certain young French Arabs, seeing that the old Republican bargain—under which you surrendered any prior or alternative allegiances in order to become a full-fledged Frenchman—was a scam, have turned to militant Islam.

And French Gypsies? What do people from St. Jacques do, if there's no way forward, no reward for becoming

"French," if, like Daniel, you graduate from the finest university and still can't find a decent job?

There are Gypsy fundamentalists, but they don't throw bombs. They don't hijack planes or blow up supertankers, they blow up themselves. They get so fat that at forty they can barely climb the stairs to their own apartment, they shoot smack and catch AIDS, they become Pentacostalist pastors preaching that the Internet is the devil's plaything, that women belong at home, that Gypsies need to return to their values, which means music, horses, cards. They forget their French and keep their children out of school and marry them to their first cousins aged fourteen. They accept bribes to vote for Mayor Alduy. They lose their teeth and are too frightened to go to the dentist. They die of minor diseases against which other French people—people who go to school—are inoculated. And they don't leave a trace.

4

For a few years, I saw less of Diane.

Writers—most writers—are opportunists: I had got my material, more than I could possibly use, and now I was burrowing deep into my warren to write it up, and I needed not to see Diane in order to be able to "see" her better.

I would phone her after four months' silence and make a date to drop by the apartment, and when I arrived, no one would be home. Later, she'd tell me that she'd gone to visit her aunt in the hospital, but I chose to take her usual remissness as justification to stay away.

The culture gap was widening. As my children got older, I found myself nagging them to practice the violin every day, drilling them for math tests, taking them from horseback-riding lessons to swimming lessons. The clash between the middle-class virtues and achievement I was striving to instill in them and the ostentatious lawlessness required of the Gypsy children with whom I took them to play got harder to explain.

Garth lent me a tape of *The Prince,* an early Tony Gatlif movie about French Gypsies. I watched it with Maud. She was appalled. "The girl's father punishes her because she wants to go to school, and because she doesn't want to steal!" Such antinomianism wasn't even intriguing to her, it was just plain awful.

Our jaunts along the malls of the Route d'Espagne, the birthday parties where men got silently drunk on orange pop and whiskey and babies in flamenco dresses were made to stand on the counter of a bar and shimmy to rumba felt like a phase I'd grown out of. My interest in the Gypsies had been voyeuristic slumming, and I hadn't been able to do Diane much good.

That's what I thought. But with another few twists of time's knife, I found it wasn't true, that we had entered into each other's hearts and lives inextricably deeply, that the first quick cycle of infatuation and disenchantment had given way to something slower, more lasting. Time, of which I thought the Gypsies had no grasp, had done its trick. The fact that Diane and Moïse and their families had all known Theo when he was an elfin, silver-blond toddler and now he was a well-built seven-year-old who preferred history books to motorcycles, and yet was still just as flamboyantly headstrong, still, as Diane wrote me in one heart-rending letter, her *petit Gitan,* that I'd played cards with Kevin when he was a pudgy third-grader and now he was a grown man old enough to marry, that we were in each other's photo albums, year after year, hugging, clowning, grinning foolishly, Moïse's beard getting grayer, me getting scrawnier, Diane getting puffier, meant that we were part of each other's family narrative.

And that when we meet, we take up where we left off.

5

These days, I ring Diane's doorbell after a long absence, and get a prodigal welcome.

After she's had her fill of me, I'm hauled around the neighborhood like a trophy. We go upstairs to visit Linda and Tanya and Mickaël; we drop by the rue des Carmes, where Antoinette feeds me a six-o'clock supper of sausages and beans, alongside her daughters and daughters-in-law; Uncle Francisquet plays me Frank Sinatra songs on the guitar and coaxes me into singing along.

Everybody's been worried about me. Antoinette says, "I tell Diane, It's not like Fernande to stay away. There must be trouble in her family, she must be sick."

Bimba, Samir's wife, who didn't used to permit herself to address me directly, declares, "Every time, I ask Diane, How's Fernande, where's Fernande, why doesn't she come by anymore?"

I give an excuse which is both true and comprehensible to these dyed-in-the-wool depressives, explaining I've been holed up at home for months, too blue even to pick up the phone.

I hear all the news: Tanya's majoring in psychology at the University of Montpellier, loving every minute of it. After a bumpy first year, she's now getting straight A's. Linda's been accepted in a business training program, and is on-again, off-again with her French boyfriend, whom Diane finds too old and slow for her.

Remember Mario, Linda's lifelong lover, father of Tanya? "I talked to Mario in Paris," says Diane, "I asked, When are you coming down to see us? He told me, Watch out, if I come, I'll make your sister another baby."

"Why not?" I wonder.

"Why not? Because he's just had another child by a *third* woman, that's why," laughs Diane.

Daniel has left the chess academy for work he loves, as a job counselor at a government unemployment agency. It's a job for life, with all the benefits of a government post, which means he's landed in the clover. He lights up when he speaks of his new work, which exercises to the full his kindness and sociability. Unfortunately, his wife, Christine, who stood by him all the years he was broke and miserable, has now left him and taken their daughter, Eve, back to her parents in Arles. Diane's version is that Christine fell in with a fast crowd, and got fed up with Daniel's not wanting to smoke dope and party every night. But you can never trust hearing just one side of a story.

Bimba and Samir now have a second daughter, Loanna, whom Childe Maëva hasn't yet murdered, and they've moved from the Caserne into the top floor of Diane and Linda's building, thus making La Fantaisie a second rue des Carmes, an outpost of modern Gypsydom. Later on, Samir, the naughtiest of the naughty, gets religion. Last I heard, he was working as a school cleaner, making half of what he earned selling counterfeit Vuitton and Nikes, and no longer going out except to escort his wife and daughters to the *Assemblée*. Bimba, Diane says, is over the moon. They have even gone to the Town Hall for a "real" wedding.

There are other marriages, too. "Remember David?"

David is the fourteen-year-old son of Moïse's brother Jérémie, a clumsy, touchingly friendly boy, still with his baby fat and just the first blush of moustache on his upper lip. "He's married."

The family thought he was a bit young, but actually, says Diane, it wasn't such a bad idea. David's father Jérémie's a drug-addict, his mother abandoned the children, David had only a grandmother who was too sick to look after him. David's father-in-law buys the young couple everything they need. "This way, he's got someone to take care of him."

Moïse's daughter, Miriam, too, is now married to her seventeen-year-old fiancé, but this is a more grievous event. The couple sneaked off and got married in secret, just before the huge wedding the two families had planned. They eloped in order to avoid the handkerchief rite, Diane tells me, since they'd already slept together. "If you're not a virgin, if you've 'ridden horseback,' the old woman takes one look and says, 'Get up, it's not worth the trouble,' and the groom's family calls off the wedding."

"Moïse cried for three days. For three days and three nights, he was in tears, he wanted to kill the boy. I calmed him down, but it's hurt his pride as a father. He wanted to do the handkerchief for his daughter. He said, 'At least she could have let me do the handkerchief, even without a big wedding,' but no." Later that year, Miriam gives birth to a son, Julian, making Moïse a grandfather at thirty-one.

Marlon is now four and a half, and is just emerging from a plague of tantrums. He has joined the men's world—Diane can suffer him no more than before—and spends his days being traded off between Kevin and Moïse, who laugh when he talks dirty or gives you the finger.

Kevin, at fourteen, is a tall, slim, handsome young man,

honey-skinned, almond-eyed, laughing, with loving kindness and courtesy that win him friends wherever he goes. Gypsy girls ask for his hand, and Moïse is longing to find him a wife among the *petites cousines* of St. Jacques, but Kevin finds the idea ludicrous. He's never had a single Gypsy friend—why would he want to marry one?

Kevin doesn't seem to go to school much anymore—he repeated two years while his mother was sick—but he's being courted by one of France's best junior league soccer teams. When I see him downtown with his old gang of friends—Banna, Isa, Mohammad—I see he's shed all traces of St. Jacques in favor of the universal homeboy mode. If he might be hard-pressed at this point to make it into the French middle-class like his cousin Tanya, I guess he never had a powerhouse mother like Linda to make him go to bed early and get straight A's.

Moïse is now 34, and eager to have some grandchildren he can consider legitimate. He says, "My time is over. By forty, I'll be sitting by the fire with my slippers and my pipe. Now it's my childrens' turn." Moïse has been in mysteriously bad health, a recurrence of the mini comas he's been prone to: he has raging headaches, he falls asleep and can't be woken, he no longer dares drive his car. The doctors are perplexed, but Moïse refuses to have any of the tests that might determine what's wrong. It's only later that I understand Moïse thinks the sickness is a sign from God telling him to repent and be born again.

6

June 2004. Maud is playing in a violin concert at the conservatory. We arrive ridiculously early. The conservatory has a broad sunny plaza into which habitués of St. Mathieu often spill over.

Today, on the steps of the conservatory, there is a group that looks as if it's been there a long time, and has nowhere else to go. A roly-poly nut-brown man, unshaven, gap-toothed, whom you might take for a vagrant, were it not for the whiteness of his dress shirt. In the dust before him, a large toddler with heavy-laden diapers sagging to his knees, a little girl wearing what once must have been a flamenco dress, and a bigger girl in hot-pink spandex.

It's Moïse's brother Salomon, who is delighted to see me. *Paios* love Salomon—even sour Guy Bertrand pronounces him a holy idiot, a natural, a wonder of guileless guiles.

I remember Garth's telling me about driving Salomon and his wife, Maza, to the clinic to visit their daughter, who, according to Garth, was brain damaged from their not having thought to feed her for the first six weeks of her life—the one who later died. While Maza was "visiting" at the clinic, Salomon asked Garth to take him to the beach, where he wanted to learn how to skip stones. I think the gist of the story was that Salomon no way could get the hang of skipping stones, but was blissed-out happy just to sit on a driftwood log, dying daughter quite forgotten.

Today, Salomon looks as if left to his own devices he might spend a similar eternity blissing out on the steps of the conservatory.

"How are you?" I ask.

"Not so well," he beams, switching over to an expression of pitiable suffering.

"What's wrong?"

"Maza, Maza. You know my wife, Maza?"

The only time I've formally met Maza, who is a wild animal, was at a Tekameli concert in a church in Port Vendres. I was there with my cousins, and after the concert, we took Moïse and Salomon and Maza for a drink at a dockside café (this being one of the times Diane and Moïse were broken up, and Moïse was thus on warmer terms with his own kin). Maza had refused to touch anything but salt and whole lemons, which she bit into and ate like an apple. When we left, Maza pocketed not only the remaining lemons, but the salt, which she funneled into the silver paper of an empty cigarette packet, eyes raking the waiters in readiness for flight.

Maza is a *toxicomane*, Salomon explains, one hand jabbing at the crook of his arm to illustrate. She will do anything for a fix! She has gone off searching for drugs and left him in the street with no money and three hungry children.

I commiserate, trying to look shocked.

Now Salomon jabs the same cupped hand toward his mouth, and toward his children's mouths, while his squinched-up eyes squeeze out tears. Three hungry children, three hungry mouths to feed. His weeping, imploring, miserable expression, his hand to the mouth are age-old Gypsy begging gestures you see the world over, archetypal as watching a dog turn around three times before lying down.

But the funny thing is, in six years of hanging around St. Jacques Gypsies, this is the first time anybody's ever hit me up for money. I figure I've got off lightly, so I head for the nearest cash machine and return with as much money as he asked for. Salomon is too much of a gentleman to show either surprise at my actually returning or regret at not having asked for more. Grinning, he enfolds me in a warm bear hug, and asks when we can meet again for a drink, a cup of coffee, can I come back that same afternoon or evening, and we even specify the exact time on the clock at which we will meet on the conservatory steps. I think how much easier it is to get along with Gypsies when neither of you is troubled by the remotest intention of keeping the date. Salomon's oldest daughter has been playing with Maud, hugging her, dancing with her, making much of her, and as we leave, Maud remarks with satisfaction, "Gypsies are so affectionate!"

When I tell Diane about this encounter, she screams with laughter. Salomon is such a cut-up—did I ever hear about the time he went to church just to get a slug of communion wine, and how when the priest then bent down to him with the proffered host, Salomon opened his mouth and let out a great belch in the priest's face? From then on, it's a running joke between me and Diane and Moïse that Salomon hit me up for money by saying that Maza was a drug addict and I was fool enough to give it.

The following week, when I run into Salomon again—at a Tekameli concert at a farm in the mountains, where Moïse dedicates a song to me because the day after tomorrow, I am leaving Roussillon, and because he himself has finally been baptized, which means he is no longer supposed to be performing profane music for a lay audience—Salomon bursts out laughing at the sight of me, and enfolds me in a still more affectionate hug. It was good fun that he fooled me into thinking Maza was a drug fiend, and good fun that I let myself be fooled.

Chapter Fourteen

1

We are throwing a massive Fourth of July going-away party, because in three days' time we are leaving Roussillon for good. It's been six years, and the owners of our house want it back, and it's time for us cuckoo parents to find a home less flimsy than a rented summerhouse.

We are leaving the Mediterranean. We have bought ourselves a big stone house with twenty acres of woods and a stream, just over the climatic watershed that divides northern France from the south, where winter begins in October and continues, with mud and sleet and snow, till April, and where land and houses are commensurately cheap.

From our future house, Perpignan will be a four-hour ride on an antiquated train full of crewcut soldiers on leave and Islamist preachers and a Berber mother and daughter with their lunch packed in a basket covered with a cloth, who offer their food to fellow-passengers before eating. You'll get out at Perpignan Station, last major stop in France before Spanish Port Bou, where Walter Benjamin committed suicide on the strength of a rumor that he was about to get sent

229

back across the border. You'll blink in the harsh sunlight, strip off your coat, marvel at the date palms, the orange blossoms, the flamingos in the lagoon, and wonder how a place so forlorn, so back-of-beyond, can feel like the home you lost.

I am so sad I can hardly stand. The last days are a river of tears, down which float cartons of books and bedsheets and saucepans and lists of all that's left undone.

2

We've invited seventy people for lunch. At 11:45 a.m., the first guests arrive. There's a stream of honking, and an aquamarine sports car followed by a battered van comes rattling into the courtyard, with shouts and whoops and shrieks—it's Moïse and Diane and Kevin and Marlon in the Kyoto, and Linda and Mickaël and Linda's French boyfriend and the boyfriend's children in the boyfriend's van.

Diane emerges with a little swagger and stops dead at the sight of me. "Fernande, you're not wearing *those* old clothes to your party? Come on, let's go upstairs and find you something a little more *moderne*. What ever happened to that leopard-skin top I gave you?"

Our going-away party is a mixed bag of friends and neighbors. There is a sampling of the local gentry, ultra-Catholic and conservative, coiffed blonde ladies with navy-blue cardigans, whose navy-blue children each have two names (Marie-Hélène, Jean-François) and whose little boys—once their parents' backs are turned—tend to be more murderous than Gypsies; there are doctors and schoolteachers, a carpenter, an army officer, a sailor and a boatbuilder, several farmers, and Stéphane, our neighbor who used to be an actor in a traveling troupe and now is a born-again Catholic who programs the diocese's computers.

There is Irish Garth from the Casa Musicale and his wife, Pascale, and their daughter, Juliette; there is Frédéric, who first took me around knocking on St. Jacques doors, and thanks to whom I met Moïse and Diane, and Frédéric's wife, Hajiba, and their daughter Aurore and Hajiba's daughter Siham. There are all our children's friends and their friends' parents.

Maud by now has left the village school, and is in a magnet program for musicians ensconced within a tough Gypsy ZEP in St. Mathieu. Her friends are a free, clever bunch, whose parents come from Brazil and Algeria and Senegal and Northern France. Our neighbor Sylvie has concocted a massive all-day treasure hunt for the children, with clues from Archimedes and Descartes.

We have lunch at long trestle tables in the garden, which need to be occasionally shifted in a serpentine conga line in flight from the brazen sun. There are grilled sardines and Catalan sausages that come in rings, and wine from the grapes in our backyard; everybody brings salads and cheeses and cakes, and some friends who run a bakery bring enough loaves to feed Jesus' multitudes, and more cakes.

It's a sweet sad day, on which emotions run high. Madame de Saint Prix, our landlord's aunt, who's eighty-three and immensely gallant, sings a Maurice Chevalier song she's modified in our honor. And Moïse starts prowling around, looking queasy with stage fright, telling anybody who'll listen that he's brought his guitar and he's planning to sing. Telling everybody, so he won't back down.

I like the way time has changed things for me and the

Gypsies. I remember back when I thought Moïse and I could never be friends. I know that in the strangest way, we are. He counts on me—aside from knowing that if Diane's with me, she's safe—he's glad I'm in his life, and he wants me to keep on being there.

There are certain of our Roussillon friends for whom we, Anglo-Americans who live in a big strange house that isn't ours, and disappear regularly to London or New York, have been strange as Gypsies, people bound by no code they recognize—whether the hours at which we eat, or the limits we don't set for our children. And yet, over the years, they have come to trust us, and now there will be a hole left where we were.

It's quite a wrench for Moïse to leave St. Jacques and get himself stranded way out in the country at a sit-down party full of *paios*. The last time he came to our house—for my birthday, two years earlier—it was winter and he'd stayed outside in the cold most of the day, and finally taken off with Garth mid-lunch in search of cigarettes.

That was the time Moïse asked Garth if he knew that Pascal Valles, the other great Tekameli vocalist, had quit the group in order to become a Pentacostalist pastor in the *Assembleé*. "And you know what?" said Moïse. "More and more, I think Pascal's on to something. Regular pay, no papers to fill out, no nights on the road—home, *tranquille*." That was eighteen months before Moïse found his own way to being baptized.

This time, Moïse is at ease, even though he's no longer allowed to have a beer or a cigarette. There are more of our friends whom he knows, and who know him. He eats his fill, he stretches out on a Turkish rug under the shade of a pine tree, with Marlon in his lap, people wander over to talk to him, and then he has a nice long snooze. When he awakens, he's ready to sing.

Moïse comes round to the table where I am sitting, and he plays and sings to me. He stands, playing his guitar and singing. Now our respectable friends, who had been puzzled by being invited to lunch with such a large group of Gypsy-Arab-Africans, people you'd normally cross a street to avoid, are somewhat mollified, since Moïse has just entered the recognizable category of hired entertainment. So, while Moïse stands and plays and sings to us, the blondes in navy blue continue eating and talking and laughing, just as if we were in a restaurant and he were hustling for spare change.

There is no way they can understand that Moïse in fact is a great singer who hates to sing, who has very little interest in music in general, for whom his "gift" is something that at times he's seen as an easy way of making money or getting girls, but that more often is awkward, shaming, even anguishing. That in fact for a long time God has been calling out, "Moses!" and that finally, shy, unsure, but willing, Moïse has answered, "Here I am," and that religion for Moïse will be a graceful way of relinquishing a profession for which he has little taste.

Moïse sang a few songs, and then, offended by the guests' continuing chatter, he stopped in the middle of a song and walked away. Everybody then felt badly at having been unmannerly, and he was persuaded to come back and sing to a chastened and more receptive audience. At first he sang a few big rumba numbers, and then he began singing his religious songs. Later, my friend Pierre told me he'd overheard Linda saying to Diane in Gitan, "Why's he wasting his time playing *canticas* to these tourists? All they're looking for is 'Bambolera' "—the Gipsy Kings' hit song. But Moïse sang his canticles because he wanted to kindle in us the love of God, and it wasn't that he sang better than usual, because his voice is surely waning from neglect, but it was the first time I'd heard Moïse sing because he wanted to.

Later on, something happens which Moïse wasn't in the least expecting. Provincial France is a place where, after a meal, people pass around a guitar and sing songs, where after your friends have sung their old chestnuts, they ask you to sing a typical song from your country. Before the war, maybe French people would have danced too, but at least they sing.

Olivier, our neighbor who's a doctor by trade, gets his two guitars, and Frédéric too has brought a guitar, and Vincent, who runs a "musical farm" where students come on vacation to pick organic vegetables and study percussion, happens to have in the back of the car his conga drums. They sit in a circle, along with Moïse, and they see what each has got on his mind, and everybody who wants to listen joins them.

Till nightfall, they sit in the garden and jam, slowly, softly, tentatively, one taking up a rhythm and just letting it dangle in the air till the others jump in, seize it, and shake it inside out, and the sound moves elsewhere.

Now it's no longer Moïse who is singing but Sara, a tall, angular Brazilian from the northern hinterland, with a strange, beautiful face narrow and anxious as fox terrier's, who lives in the Pyrenean foothills with her husband and their two children.

Sara, like Moïse, is a "savage," as she puts it, who doesn't like to sing in front of other people. When she sings, she has the saddest voice you can imagine, full of orphaned fragments and lonesome ellipses and undertones and silences that make everyone who hears her draw closer and stiller.

All afternoon, Moïse plays guitar for Sara, and she listens to the unfamiliar rhythms, beating time on her long sinewy thigh, and then she jumps in and improvises lyrics to his flamenco-ized rumba, inventing songs in Portuguese about how we are all here at Fernanda's *casa,* and then Moïse adds a little in Gitan. As in the sweetest encounters, neither understands what the other one's saying, and it doesn't matter.

I have never seen Moïse drawn out of himself, and open to something new. I've never seen Moïse sense that music is not just a finite hand-me-down you're born with, but something various, changeable, other, to fly after with both hands open. I know I will never see it again.

3

In September 2004, Garth sends me a clipping from the local newspaper. It's a brief article about a young woman living in the remote mountain village of Prat de Mollo, who's been murdered by her ex-boyfriend. The twenty-seven-year-old victim is from a local French Catalan family who had recently returned to the area. The young woman worked in an after-school program for children, her mother was deputy mayor in charge of youth and education; the family belonged to all the local clubs. "They were the kind of people who bring life to a remote village," the mayor of Prat de Mollo was quoted as saying. The murdered woman was the mother of a three-year-old daughter.

The murderer, who was found in the street outside her house and at once confessed to "the facts," was an outsider. Although he was the father of her child, nobody in the village seemed to know him. He was "a man of the name of

Espinasse [sic], a Perpignanais belonging to the community of travelers."

The unnamed Espinas, I learn from Garth's letter, is Moïse and Solomon's brother, Jérémie, father not just of the orphaned *"fillette"* but also of Nelly and of David, who was said to be well-off marrying at fourteen because that way at least he would have someone to look after him. The article's tone is of decent outrage. "One of us," from good people, pillars of the community, has been cut down in cold blood by "one of them," leaving an innocent three-year-old orphaned. What do you expect, from *"gens du voyage"*?

4

That winter, I come back to Roussillon to see Diane. She is sitting in the shuttered darkness of the apartment. She is swollen from all the drugs she takes, and can no longer get about much. She has just had an operation on her herniated disk, which she thinks didn't work, and she wishes she could cut back on the morphine, but she can't. Someday she will get the strength, but not now. She thinks back on the days we used to romp around downtown, shopping for stilettos, running after the carnival floats, throwing confetti at strangers. Now she can't even drag herself downstairs.

Moïse is off "buying Coca-Cola." Moïse isn't playing anymore, she tells me. Maybe at a wedding or a baptism he'll sing, but only canticles. For a long time Diane was telling him, "Moïse, you can't live with a foot in each world. If you don't sing, we don't eat." (The ant's advice, after all, was not so far off the mark.) Now Moïse has chosen to land with both feet in the Other World, the world of men in black suits.

Now all they have to live on is welfare and handouts from Diane's mother, whose husband, Tony, earns good money as an accountant at a fruit transportation center.

On the table where they used to play gin rummy there's now a child's Bible, a French translation of a dumbed-down American Good News Bible, with illustrations and different-colored print, and a table of contents telling you where to find what you're looking for—the healing of a sick person, a homily about good husbandry. I see from the inscriptions on the frontispiece that this Bible has been handed from Gypsy child to Gypsy child—it belonged to Isaie, and to Abraham, and to Elie, and now it's Moïse's, but he hasn't written his name in it.

Marlon wants to look at the Bible, but Diane swats him away. "Hands off, that's your papa's."

I suddenly wonder if finding God isn't Moïse's most ingenious way of driving Diane up the wall.

"I've been depressed since you left, Fernande," she tells me. "I've even talked to the social worker about it—how bad I feel since you moved away, how one thing after another gets me down."

Worst of all has been this business with Jérémie. People are saying he killed his girlfriend, Marie, because she wouldn't give him any more money to score drugs. In fact, Diane says, it was Marie who was always hitting up Jérémie for money.

"I used to tell Marie to leave him alone. She'd take Jérémie back for three days, pocket his money, and throw him out again. He slashed her face one time with his knife—she had a scar all down one cheek. I said, Marie, stay away from him. One night I went to the ladies' room at Auchan, I hadn't seen Marie for a couple of years; I see a girl. I said, Marie is that you? She said, Have you heard the news?

Jérémie and I are back together again. I said, Marie, you better watch what you do, because you can't keep on playing that same old trick on Jérémie. She said, No, this time's for real; he's going into detox to dry up, and when he gets out, we're getting married."

First week or so, Diane says, Marie comes to see him every day. Then silence. Jérémie checks himself out of the clinic. Without telling anybody, he goes up to the mountains to her house.

"He wants to slash her face, like last time, but she jerks her head away"—Diane indicates just how—"and the knife catches her throat.

"You know I'm not a judging person, Fernande, but I don't have it in me to forgive Jérémie for taking that girl's life. Moïse goes to see Jérémie in prison. He asks me to write letters for him to send to Jérémie—you know Moïse can't write. I tell him, Mo, I can't.

"Jérémie will do six, eight years of prison maybe, and then he'll be free. But Marie will never be free. Their baby daughter will never have her mother back. I say, Mo, Don't ask me to write him. I can't forgive him yet."

For Diane, the crime is purely personal. She doesn't think to blame Jérémie for having involuntarily confirmed French people's worst prejudices about Gypsies, for having undone all Moïse's efforts to create a more honorable image of Gypsies as world-famous musicians, men of the Church.

Marlon is at her elbow, wanting to know what we're talking about, and she says, "Nothing, baby." He runs to the refrigerator, grabs himself a Coke, cries because there are no more cookies. When he hears his aunt Bimba going up the stairs, he wants to go play with his cousin Loanna. "Shut up, you get on my nerves," Diane snaps. Marlon pads away, grumbling.

Later, Diane discovers that Marlon's been scribbling all over the school photograph of Kevin that Kevin's given me, industriously scrubbing out every trace of his older brother's smiling face. Diane tells Marlon he's a bad kid and whacks him hard, and his face crumples into a weeping mess of horror, humiliation, disbelief. Even if Diane hit Marlon a hundred times and told him every day he was bad, each time it would shock him as much as if it had never happened before. It takes a long time for his last whimper to die away.

Diane, sighing, hobbles over to the stereo and puts on a demo of the last few songs Tekameli ever made—a mix of rumba, reggae, and even Balkan Gypsy chants, in which you hear the old magic undiminished.

"My God, Fernande, how beautiful their voices are," she murmurs, husky.

The apartment is dark. She is sitting at the table, in white sateen pajamas and fluffy bedroom slippers, beating time with her small, plump, nail-bitten hand. She sings along to Tekameli in her hoarse broken voice, translating into French for me the Spanish and Gitan lyrics.

"Put your trust in God, let Him into your heart, open yourself up to God, He will always help you," she croaks sweetly.

Her face is a boy's face, with big rough features. There are deep black circles under her eyes, her large nose looks broken from a dozen fistfights, she is missing a few teeth and those that remain are rotting. Her face is the face of urban poverty—of orphans, beggars, refugees, "unwanteds" the world over—a face that transplanted, say, to contemporary Manhattan, you would only see in a homeless shelter or a halfway house. When you first meet Diane, she looks scary, but then you discover something infinitely moving in her sweet grin, a common sense and quick humanity hiding beneath her apparent wackiness.

She is singing to me the last songs Tekameli's ever likely to record, while she points up to heaven with her forefinger. She's knocking on her heart with her fist, tears are flooding down her cheeks.

"You know," she says, "when Moïse signed the Sony contract, we got money and we blew it all—we bought the car, we bought the furniture, and now we're broke.

"I love to spend money, it gives me a good feeling in my heart to run through it fast. I always have friends, family who come to me saying, I'm hungry, and even when I have nothing, I take them out to a restaurant and order everything on the menu. So what if we won't eat tomorrow? Because God who sees everything knows I do good, that I give to anybody who needs it, when I have nothing myself." She points again to the sky. "Believe me, Fernande. Even if no one else is looking, God sees everything."

5

It seems as if there's a battle of the angels being waged in Gypsy St. Jacques. On the one hand, there's the familiar war between fundamentalism and modernity, which is essentially a question of control, whether political or familial ("If my daughter learns to read, she will escape"). And then there's the internal struggle within hard-core Gypsydom, an old-fashioned, big-tent revivalist bang-up between Satan and redemption, between the men in black with healing hands and the men who still drink and smoke and shoot smack and knife their girlfriends, a war in which women have little to gain either way.

Somehow I know that when Jérémie starts serving his time, there will be a chaplain waiting for him—whether Jeannot's father, who's saved whole families of drug addicts, or a younger breed of spiritual entrepreneur—who will bring him to Jesus, and when he gets out, Jérémie will no longer be this will-o'-the-wisp you see wandering the lower streets of St. Jacques in a trembling dream, but a plump personable man in black suit and white shirt who tells you, hand on heart, that we're all God's children, whether French or Gypsy or purple or green.

When I go back to Perpignan now, the city too looks plumper and more personable. The FNAC entertainment complex has opened in the old Belle Epoque department store. There's a sushi bar in the Place de la République. In St. Jacques, tumbledown houses are getting renovated by the mayor's office, and you just know that once they're all beautiful, nobody will want to stick Gypsies back in them.

Perpignan is still the end of the line, a border-town of refugees, outcasts, and derelicts. There are still more public scribes and button stores than day spas. But the new demographics of migrant labor, in which Eastern Europeans and, increasingly, Asians are replacing the old Spanish, Portuguese, and North African workforce, are making Perpignan's underclass feel less distinctively Mediterranean.

For this year's *vendange*, Georges de Massia, the manager of the vineyard on which we used to live, hired, instead of the usual band of poor French and Arab roustabouts, a team of young Chinese women. He told me, marveling, how quiet, efficient, industrious these women were. There were no noonday feasts at trestle tables in the sun, no drinking, no singing, no knife fights, no wisecracks about how bad the wine was, and when their work was done, they got on their bikes and headed back to Perpignan, where doubtless they worked a second job. Next year, there are going to be twice as many Chinese working Roussillon's vineyards, and nobody's going to be left to sing the old songs grape-pickers from Burgundy to Collioure sing to make the work go sweeter.

Already it seems as if there are fewer Gypsies in downtown Perpignan than there used to be, and the young Gypsies you see are as likely to be wearing tracksuits as zoot suits. For the first time, I wonder if, in even five years' time, there will still be brindle roosters and fat girls in silk pajamas parading around Place Puig on a weekday afternoon, and "O Madre" wailing from an upstairs window.

A Note About the Author

Fernanda Eberstadt is the author of four novels. She lives in France with her husband and two children.

A Note on the Type

This book was set in Galliard, a typeface drawn by Matthew Carter for the Mergenthaler Linotype Company in 1978.

Composed by Creative Graphics
Allentown, Pennsylvania

Printed and bound by R.R. Donnelley & Sons
Harrisonburg, Virginia

Designed by Pamela G. Parker